Having spent more than 25 years […], I recognized many of the anecdotes i[…] to read, it gives a reflective account of […]se of realism. Looking beyond IT proj[…]ity in all projects, whilst not necessarily having to give them the label of an agile project. It gives a balanced view by comparing and contrasting the views of the APM, PMI and Prince. I endorse this book for those at the start of their careers about to start working on projects, project professionals already managing projects (agile or otherwise) and those responsible for creating the environments in which projects exist. For me, *Agile Beyond IT* addresses several key misconceptions and learnings about agile, which include: SCRUM is not an agile project management framework; agile is not a silver bullet; agile projects still need a PMO and risk cannot be ignored but we could stand a bit closer to the cliff edge by letting project professionals use their judgment; and finally being allowed to fail early saves cost and embarrassment. My key take-away from the book is there are two important ingredients to being agile: environment and people. Recognizing both of these will still need tools and processes.

Stephen Jones – Sellafield Ltd

Adrian clearly and powerfully explains how to make the organization more agile. He stresses the need for adaptation and improvement of cultural values and the policies, assumptions, practices, standards, structure, relationships and beliefs that inform and influence that culture. His book focuses on people and the agile processes that support that journey. Highly recommended.

Brian Wernham CEng, ChPP – Author of *Agile Project Management for Government*

Adrian's book is well-written, and an interesting and easy read. Illustrating explanations of ideas, principles, approaches, etc with real-life examples is always helpful, and this book is rich with these. As a P3 Assurance Professional, I particularly like his emphasis on the importance of assurance in agile projects as being no less than in 'traditional' non-agile projects, just like any other component of project management. The reader may also be interested in the APM guide 'Guide to the Assurance of Agile Delivery', for which Adrian was an important contributor.

Roy Millard – Founder and former chair of APM Assurance SIG and owner of P3 Risk & Assurance

Read this book if you are thinking of changing your organisation to use agile techniques. It describes the mindset, in readable text, you will need from Board, sponsors and project managers and provides examples to support this.

Roger Garrini RPP FAPM – chairman at APM Midlands, secretary APM Governance SIG and chair of Wolverton Town CC.

Having worked on projects and improving project management for over 40 years, I have encountered both bad and good examples of 'agility', albeit we may not have used the 'A' word. Adrian pulls the covers off the preoccupation with agile being the domain of IT and places it firmly in the business context. He explains that SCRUM is not project management and demonstrates that good project management structure and practice is still a fundamental enabler. But it's the way it is applied and the mindset of those involved that generates successful outcomes.

As well as providing good advice and examples to project managers on being more agile, Adrian also tackles the thorny stakeholder and governance issues. He suggests how those that are on the periphery of the project action, but fundamental to its success, need to view projects through a different lens. Those responsible for governance need to establish a supportive culture, focus on value and outcomes more than outputs, be comfortable with less predictability, champion empowerment, allow trial and error and encourage flexibility. Adrian shows how rigid adherence to process and methodology (as surely that gives a predictable outcome?) and 'what I did on my last project' has been shown to not deliver success.

I commend this book to all project practitioners to adopt Adrian's more adaptive approach and reap the benefits from increased agility to deliver more successful project outcomes.

Martin Samphire FAPM – former chair of APM Governance SIG, owner of 3pmxl Ltd and associate director of Deepteam

A must read for anyone wanting to apply agile to their next project! Adrian's book is highly insightful, engaging, and a delight to read through his ability to bring to life agile concepts through his extensive and rich experience stemming from the world of agile project management and beyond. It is a breath of fresh air and a much-needed addition to the project manager's toolkit in order to overcome challenges and leverage the benefits of agile project management beyond IT.

Dr Nicholas Dacre – associate professor of project management and director of the Advanced Project Management Research Centre, University of Southampton, UK

Adrian's book is a strong attempt to welcome the project manager that has seen 'agile' simply as hocus pocus to listen to some of the benefits offered via numerous simple examples. I don't see him as an 'agilist' on a holy war (and there are a few); instead he really wants to share what he's learned. Points that I noted: he concludes that a project manager equipped to be agile will be able to carry out good project management; and also recognises that projects need an integrated approach within an organizational hinterland – organizations which need to be prepared to take on a journey to improve rather than expect magic somehow to happen. And the best part: I can hear Adrian's voice reading it!

David Dunning – founder of Core P3M Data Club CIC, co-founder of Deepteam and chairman of Corporate Project Solutions

Adrian takes agile back to its roots and original principles and brings practicality to a subject that is sometimes seen with an air of mystery and as an excuse to avoid project control and rigour. Adrian dispels this myth, having been there and done it (and with the scars to prove it!) and provides lived experiences to bring the principles of agile to life. He demonstrates that agile delivery and agility live in harmony with traditional project delivery methods, showing it is not one or the other, but in fact both, living in harmony.

If you want to understand how to deliver projects more successfully and how to combine traditional and agile approaches, this is a very smart choice. I thoroughly recommend Adrian's book and only wish I'd had this evidence at my fingertips some years ago!

Lara Taylorson BSc (Hons) ChPP RPP FAPM AMICE – director of L S Taylorson Consulting Ltd

Successful projects are about giving people what they meant. Not what they wanted or needed.

Successful project people make sure they are a significant and influential part of those conversations.

It is a combination of mindset and toolset. Mostly mindset. You've got to know the rules and have the confidence to break the rules if it means getting to what is meant rather than just what is specified. So often the purpose of the project, the vision, is absent.

Project and programme people still hide behind the precise delivery of scope when they know that it is not what is meant. Which is also an abdication of the duty of care that an 'expert' or 'experienced' professional should always bring to their work rather than as a chargeable extra that allows major change order revenue to be identified and generated.

2022 is the centennial year of the polar explorer Shackleton who consistently adapted to survive and preserve the wellbeing of all involved. On the other hand, Captain Scott adhered rigorously to his scope and left us with a very detailed account of the accident.

Read and reflected upon, I believe Adrian's experience and knowledge will at the very least reassure you that it is better to be Shackleton and live to tell the tale. It is stories that change how we think and which give us the permission to act. Above all to help us to dispel the mania to adhere to methods with no regard to purpose.

Steve Wake – former chair of APM, chair of BSI MS/2 Project Programme Portfolio Standards, Freeman Worshipful Company of Educators

Having worked with Adrian many times over my career, I am not in the least bit surprised by how easy this book is to read and digest. Even more importantly it addresses a challenge that is faced by most companies today - how do I maximize my resources to ensure I create value and ultimately stay ahead of the competition?! Being able to be agile as a business is key in my opinion and Adrian has very clearly shown how organisations can evolve and adapt to a new world of 'projectisation'. As a business that is going through a shift to being an 'agile organisation' driven by 'projectisation', I recognise a lot of what is in the book in a real-life context. For me, I think this book goes way beyond projects, and rather is helping us look holistically at the new evolving businesses that demand agility to be successful. I highly recommend it to any C-level struggling with how to make their business more 'fleet of foot'!

Lee Grant – CEO Wrangu Integrated Risk, Security and Privacy Solutions

AGILE
Beyond IT

How to develop agility in project management in any sector

Adrian Pyne

First published in Great Britain by Practical Inspiration Publishing, 2022

© Adrian Pyne, 2022

The moral rights of the author have been asserted

ISBN   9781788603270   (print)
        9781788603287   (epub)
        9781788603294   (mobi)

All rights reserved. This book, or any portion thereof, may not be reproduced without the express written permission of the author.

Every effort has been made to trace copyright holders and to obtain their permission for the use of copyright material. The publisher apologizes for any errors or omissions and would be grateful if notified of any corrections that should be incorporated in future reprints or editions of this book.

Want to bulk-buy copies of this book for your team and colleagues? We can introduce case studies, customize the content and co-brand *Agile Beyond IT: How to develop agility in project management in any sector* to suit your business's needs.

Please email info@practicalinspiration.com for more details.

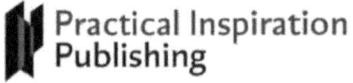

Contents

List of figures..*xi*

Foreword..*xiii*

Preface...*xv*

Introduction... 1
   How is the book structured?..4
   What this book is built on 6

Chapter 1: Adapting the principles of agility to projects................ 7
   How does agility deliver *value*?...7
   The Agile Manifesto – the foundation of agile............................9
   Adapting the Agile Manifesto to projects..................................13

Chapter 2: Setting the scene for project agility 21
   Lean vs. agile..21
   People, Process and Tools...22
   Project and organization 26
   How far should an organization go to accommodate projects? 29
   There is nothing wrong with 'traditional' project management... 29

**Chapter 3: The five most dangerous assumptions about
       project agility** 31
   Scrum isn't project management...32
   Agile projects must be iterative...34
   Agile means leaving stuff out 36
   C-suite does not 'get' agile 40
   Senior management are insufficiently engaged 43

Chapter 4: Conditions for being agile...45
   Organizational culture – the project and agility
   killer – or enabler 46
   Organizational culture – the agility killer 49
   Organizational culture – when it enables projects to *thrive* 50

Organizational project management and the project economy ... 53
Avoiding the governance vs. assurance confusion 55

Chapter 5: Adapting project management for agility – People 57
Setting the scene 57
Agility means integration 58
Culture and behaviour 61
Changing the culture for agility 64
Leadership and professionalism 67
Agile leaders' mindset 67
Hands-off leadership 70
Virtual leadership 77
Agility in project teams 82
The self model 87
Roles and responsibilities 89
Agility and creativity 89
Stakeholder management and communications 91
Resourcing and talent management 101
A talent for agility 103

Chapter 6: Adapting project management for agility – Process 105
Governance 105
Strategy and business planning 106
Approvals 108
Oversight 109
Planning, monitoring and reporting 109
Risk and issue management and problem solving 117
Change control 126
Business case and financial control 129
Financial control 134
Resource management 136
Third party management and agile contracts 138
Quality management 146
Roles and responsibilities 149

**Chapter 7: Adapting project management for agility –
Tools and AI 151**
The journey to AI 151
Spoilt for choice – choosing software tools 152
Tools and project management maturity 153
Single or multiple tools? 154

Tools, reporting and communication 155

Chapter 8: Adapting project management for agility – Portfolios and programmes 157
Agility and programme management 157
Facing outwards – the programme and organization 157
Facing inwards 159
Programme shaping 160
Programme delivery 161
Agility and portfolio management 163
Organizational agility and portfolio management 163
Permanent portfolios 164
Portfolios and the business planning cycle 165
Building an agile portfolio 166
Managing an agile portfolio 170
Agility and the PMO 174

Chapter 9: Becoming agile… at projects 177
How agile are you prepared to be? 177
Vision, mission and strategy for project agility 178
Winning the C-suite and other stakeholders 179
Avoiding the pitfalls 181
Not throwing the baby out with the bathwater 182
An agile project management maturity model 183
Roadmap to agility 188

Chapter 10: Conclusions 191

Appendix 193
  Learn more about lean vs. agile 193

Acknowledgements 197

About the author 199

Glossary 201

Notes 205

Index 207

Figures

I.1	Book structure	5
1.1	Value from agility	7
1.2	Generic project life-cycle	14
2.1	Lean process flow	21
2.2	The iron triangle	23
2.3	The iron pyramid	24
2.4	A project's landscape	26
2.5	Project as a virus in an organization's body	27
3.1	A typical Scrum diagram	32
3.2	An IT-enabled project containing scrum	33
3.3	Aspects of project management	34
3.4	Generic project life-cycle	35
3.5	An IT-enabled project containing scrum	35
3.6	Commercial house build schedule	36
3.7	Kotter's eight-stage model for change	42
4.1	Project as a virus in the organization's body	45
4.2	A project's landscape	46
4.3	The organizational culture iceberg	49
4.4	A view of the Shell integrated project approach	51
4.5	Outline OrgPM Framework™	54
5.1	People, Process, Tools model	57
5.2	People aspects of project management	59
5.3	Process aspects of project management	59
5.4	Tools supporting project management	60
5.5	Project management framework for agility	61
5.6	The organizational culture iceberg	62
5.7	The emotional scale and the response to 'new'	64
5.8	Change management cycle	65
5.9	7Ss organization design model	66
5.10	Supermarket check-out	72
5.11	Drivers and enablers for virtual working	78
5.12	Real-life relationships	84
5.13	Finding the agile team	85

5.14	The self model	88
5.15	Stakeholder management framework	92
5.16	Stakeholder influence and interest	94
5.17	Communications planning cycle	95
5.18	BT PhONEday communications plan key components	96
5.19	BT PhONEday social media impact on costs	97
5.20	Stakeholder management vs. engagement	101
6.1	Where a business case is and is not required	131
6.2	Assess risk appetite	132
6.3	Financial controls in a supportive vs. unsupportive environment	135
6.4	Resource management	138
6.5	Saturn V rocket	146
6.6	Stage gate process	148
7.1	Tools supporting project management	151
8.1	The phases of the PoS programme	161
8.2	VMOST model	167
8.3	MoSCoW prioritization	169
9.1	Integrated model for project agility	177
9.2	Value from agile	180
9.3	Capability Management Maturity Model	183
9.4	Agile CMMM: People	186
9.5	Agile CMMM: Process	188
9.6	Agile CMMM: Tools	188
A.1	Lean process flow	193
A.2	Six Sigma model	195

Foreword

I remember being a newly qualified project manager, having attended a course and obtained a certificate but with no real-world experience. I wished that there was some guidance I could turn to apart from always disturbing my more experienced colleagues.

As I learnt more, I came to realize that project management is not really about following a set of rules but dealing with challenges and situations. Planning *is* important but being able to react to change and dealing with issues before they become major is at the heart of successful projects.

Adrian's book would have helped me enormously had it been available at the time. It is an excellent advanced book on project management because it concentrates on how to lead a successful project, not by any formal methods (although these are still important), but by the style of leadership and interactions with all stakeholders, be they the customer, a project member or a senior executive. I enjoyed the many war stories throughout the book as they highlight both successes and failures in real-life situations.

The other major challenge for project managers today is the advent of Agile. In fact, in the early days, the Agile community thought the project management discipline was not needed. Thankfully, that thinking is changing, due in part to the failure of some Agile initiatives because of lack of project management. For a project manager, however, there is the question of how to lead Agile initiatives in a way that allows the Agile principles to flourish. For instance, being able to embrace change and adapt as necessary, empowering teams to deliver value, collaboration between and active involvement of all stakeholders.

What does this mean for the project manager? Are there a totally new set of rules to follow? Do they need to forget everything they've learnt?! This book shows that embracing Agile is not an onerous task for good project managers. In fact, most of the project management principles remain safely intact. Adrian rightly shows that it is mainly a question of attitude and mindset rather than any new method. For instance, planning knowing that the plan will change. He gives valuable hints and tips on how to be more agile as well as real-life experiences with both good and bad outcomes.

This book is a useful addition to any project manager's armoury as it lets the reader benefit from the author's vast project management experience and also provides practical guidance to shifting to a more agile mindset when leading projects. I enjoyed it very much.

Steve Messenger
CEO, Agile Trainer, Coach and Consultant
Former Chair of the Agile Business Consortium

Preface

> **An apocryphal story**
>
> An Apollo mission to the moon is about 30 minutes to lift-off. There is a continual stream of interchanges between the crew in the lunar module atop the giant Saturn 5 rocket and mission control. During a short lull, the captain muses to mission control:
>
> *'Here we are sitting on top of the biggest firework ever built, consisting of about 80,000 components ALL built to minimum specification.'*
>
> Fortunately, to paraphrase President Kennedy, they landed a man on the moon and returned him successfully to the earth.

Not only was that one of the best project visions of all time, but the means of achievement reflected a philosophy of agility. Do things *just good enough*. If those 80,000 specifications were fit for purpose, there was no need, no point, no waste in cost, time or sweat to build them any better.

Fast forward to early in 2021 when I was asked, not for the first time, if there was a book about agile project management that was not focused on software projects. I was motivated to write one.

This book is for anyone involved in projects, from the Board through all levels of project professionals, to those who find themselves involved in projects, would like to be, or are studying management.

It is for anyone who wants to see what agility looks like from the viewpoint of project management practices rather than the perspective of the type of project (such as marketing, engineering, construction). Especially if your experience, or reading, is of software development projects, notably those using agile development frameworks such as Scrum.

No matter what industry you are in, from aviation, engineering, mining, retail and many others, whether private or the public sector, this book will help you to see how agility in project management can work for you.

I will not ignore IT-enabled projects, programmes and portfolios, but I'll demonstrate that there is so much more to project agility than IT.

Introduction

This book is for anyone who wants to use agility to get value from projects more often and more reliably.

Agility seems to be one of the buzzwords of our times. The incredible rise of companies like Amazon and Uber, together with many disruptor companies such as those in the financial sector, is often attributed to their agility. The business press frequently run articles on the need for organizations to become agile to remain competitive. And agile frameworks dominate IT.

For me, the key driver for agility is to become more successful in delivering projects, and so get more value from them. Which is why we do projects.

However, agility is not a magic bullet and nor is it easy to achieve. But it can enable a much-needed step change in project performance, if done correctly. I say much needed as most studies I have seen over my 30-something-year career have shown that overall project performance rates have consistently maintained a range of 40–60% even across sectors.

Yes, that is four to six million pounds in every ten million wasted.

Not that the profession has stood still in that period, as I will later show. Unfortunately, it does seem that the rise in the level of project-based activity, plus their increasing scope and complexity, has left general performance unchanged. Something else is needed to achieve a step-change improvement.

The wealth of studies from academic research, Garter, Standish, professional bodies and elsewhere frequently finds recurring factors, as will be shown in Chapter 2. For now, I will just say that they can be grouped as:

a) Failures of people (mostly behavioural), of process and of technology use.
b) Failures inside projects and in the organizations around them.

Turn that on its head and you will find organizations who do gain great value from projects due to high performance with around 90% success rates. What they have in common are their approaches that address both a) and b) above. Their ways of working often reflect agility, *whether they set out to do so or not*, as I will show in some of my examples. They also demonstrate an organization that is supportive of projects, which helps them to *thrive*.

This is not new. In writing this book, I recall probably my first project in 1986 where the empowered, collaborative team were recognizably agile. We just did not describe it so and were in any case quite unaware of the term.

The drivers then for this book and for agility in projects are two-fold:

- Organizations that fail to embrace agility broadly are likely to suffer, perhaps in market share and certainly in performance.
- That agility can be the framework in which a step change in project performance and hence value delivery can be achieved.

This begs the question: is there, or rather, can there be, such a thing as agile project management?

Yes, because you can adapt agility to project management, which is what the core of this book will do.

A word of caution. This is not a new and different project management, which some have tried to claim. There is no clear blue water between project management agility and any project management method, framework or body of knowledge I know of.

So-called agile project management contains *all* the same components as other project, programme or portfolio management.

The difference with agility is in how you go about doing and using those components.

A red Ferrari is a Ferrari… that is red. Agile project management is project management… done in an agile way.

Steve Messenger, former Chair of the Agile Business Consortium, says that *agile is a state of mind.* Which scares the life out of many, especially in the C-suite. *Invest in a mindset? Are you mad?* And agility does require organizations to modify themselves to make it work.

Agility may be fashionable, but it is real and relates well to two other major emerging trends in project management: the *projectization* of work and artificial intelligence (AI).

The projectization of work, which the Project Management Institute (PMI) has reflected in the term *the project economy*, recognizes that how organizations operate in respect of projects is a critical factor in performance, much ignored until recently. This concept seeks to end the fallacy that an organization can run two separate universes – the business-as-usual universe and the project universe. The latter being very much the poor relation. Instead, it sees them as the Yin and Yang of a new operation. They need to be integrated through strategic and business planning and leadership, dependent on each other. I will describe this using a model called *organizational project management.*

The other trend, AI, also to be discussed in the book, has the potential to greatly automate parts of project management. It provides real-time information, trends and predictions, and enables project professionals to spend more time managing that most difficult of project disruptors – people.

The relationship between agility, the project economy and AI lies in their integration into a holistic project approach. Thinking again about organizations that are good at projects, they have integrated approaches. This book will show what that looks like and how to build and sustain it.

Where does agility come from?

There is no simple answer to this question as agility is a river that has risen from many tributaries. One such is Kanban, or Lean manufacturing, devised at Toyota in the 1940s for car manufacture. This book will base its agility on another source, the *Agile Manifesto*. This was defined in 2001 by 17 software engineering experts, who sought to move away from documentation-heavy bureaucratic development methods to become more *lean*, more... agile.

Since then, the Agile Manifesto has caused agility to become compelling. Why?

1. Agility is a byword for flexibility, which has become the holy grail for many organizations who do not want to fall to sector disruptors and go the way of buggy whip makers. Covid-19 being the latest and quite appalling disruptor.
2. The Agile Manifesto is well defined, ably depicts what being agile is and is broadly recognized. Its principles are coherent and may be readily adapted beyond their software development origins. Which leads naturally to...

3. Adapting the Agile Manifesto to project management provides a coherent, holistic framework, not just at the project (and programme and portfolio) level, but also for the organizational hinterland of projects. That is, what an organization needs to do to build and sustain successful agile projects.

All of this means that:

4. It is straightforward to demonstrate the potential considerable value of project agility to an organization, its customers, leaders and people.

Which is ironic, as focus on value is arguably the most important agile principle.

Alas, the Agile Manifesto is also an Achilles' heel. Many folk cannot separate agile from software development. Very many books and guides on so-called agile project management are eloquent on the management of agile software development projects. However, little or no distinction is drawn between what is project management and what is a software development. They emphatically are not the same thing. This is a common and very expensive mistake, for which agility, rather than its misuse, gets the blame.

For project management agility to be useful, it needs to be applicable and adaptable to projects in *any* field, from marketing to mining, and even construction. This book takes project agility ***beyond IT***.

This book then is for anyone who wishes to:

- understand what project agility looks like;
- develop great project professionals;
- or build and sustain an integrated, high-performing project delivery capability in your organization.

The final bullet is likely to result in new operations where projects can *thrive* and deliver *value*. More on this in Chapters 5 and 6.

How is the book structured?

The main body of this book is contained in Chapters 5, 6, 7 and 8.

Figure I.1 provides an overview of the book to allow you to quickly find what you may be interested in.

Introduction 5

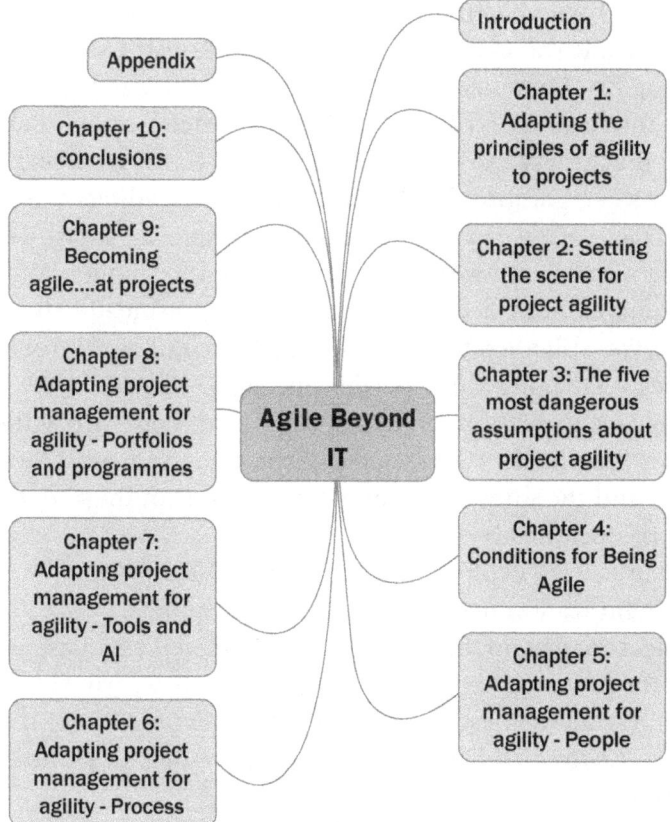

Figure I.1: Book structure

Chapter 1 shows what benefits organizations can get out of agility – being agile – and explains what agility is in terms of the Agile Manifesto's four values and 12 principles. It then describes what those values and principles look like when adapted to project management.

Chapter 2 sets the scene through comparing *Lean* and *agile* as they have much in common. The major components of a framework for project agility are outlined for later expansion. Then the relationship between projects and the organizational landscape around them is introduced, which plays a key role in project agility.

Chapter 3 describes the key traps to avoid and the myths associated with project agility.

Apart from the myths about agile, there are a number of things that some just get completely wrong, so there will be a few stories to put you on your guard.

Chapter 4 further explores the relationship between projects and organizations. It shows how and why this relationship is critical to success with agility. Organizational cultures that either threaten agility or help it to thrive are described. This leads to a description of an emerging trend that agility can help with: the projectization of work.

Chapters 5–8 get into the detail. Under the headings of *People, Process and Tools*, with a chapter for each, we examine what the project management toolbox looks like when adapted for agility. We will look at everything from project organization, roles and leadership to planning – yes, you still need to plan under agile – change control and even stage gates, managing third parties and agile contracts. We will also look at how software tools and emerging AI can help with agility. Then in Chapter 8 agility in relation to programmes and portfolios will be described, and the source of so much misunderstanding: adaptation to different project life-cycles.

In *Chapter 9* we explore and show how to *become* agile at projects. What an organization needs to do to achieve value. There's an outline agile project management maturity model as well as a basic roadmap to agility for projects. Spoiler alert: never throw the baby out with the bathwater. It's always best to build on good practices where they exist.

Finally, *Chapter 10* brings everything together and draws six key conclusions from the book.

What this book is built on

One of the many wise lessons from Eric Abrahamson in his seminal book, *Change Without Pain*,[1] is not to throw the baby out with the bath water; it's better to build on the good stuff.

This book builds on two bits of good stuff: *The Agile Manifesto* (the nearest thing I have found to a definitive reference) and the Association for Project Management's *Body of Knowledge* (BoK) 7, which helps ensure my writing is as consistent and relevant to common practice as possible.

Chapter 1

Adapting the principles of agility to projects

How does agility deliver *value*?

Business leaders are recognizing a significant body of evidence for the value of agility – whether in becoming an agile organization or for specific areas of activity, such as software development or project management.

The 2021 report by PA Consulting: *The Evolution of the Agile Organisation*,[2] showed that the top 10% of financial performers are 30% more agile than the rest. Also, organizational agility was identified as one of the top three success factors by surveyed executives, according to the Project Management Institute's 2020 Pulse of the Profession® report: *Ahead of the Curve: Forging a Future-Focused Culture*.[3]

Figure 1.1 shows the kinds of benefits that can come from agility.

Figure 1.1: Value from agility

8 Agile Beyond IT

A common story in the media, and not just the business press, is talk of disruptor companies and of digital business such as Amazon. Agility is at the heart of their operating models. Then there are the stories such as the *Economist* article in October 2021, which accused some UK businesses, long seen as 'blue chip', of being hidebound… slow to change. Anything but agile.

Add to that the views of Julian Birkinshaw, Professor of Strategy and Entrepreneurship at the London Business School. He uses the term *adhocracy* as an action-based view of the organization focused on capturing opportunities, solving problems and getting results – i.e. creating value in whatever terms that means for an organization. This description fits the disruptors, the Amazons and Ubers, of the commercial world.

In 2016 at the Drucker Forum in Vienna, Julian Birkinshaw made the provocative claim that 'We are living in the Age of Agile'. The characteristics of agility fit well into an adhocracy. Therefore, where organizations are creating or re-creating themselves as adhocracies, they will inevitably be agile.

Adhocracy and agile go together like apple pie and custard, bacon and eggs, Ginger Rogers and Fred Astaire (if you're under 60 I suggest googling them, Fred and Ginger that is).

Contrast that with the following story.

 Culture too toxic for agility

Some years ago, I was asked to speak to a UK financial institution. No names, sorry. They were interested in moving agility beyond their IT department where it was being applied successfully. I initially surveyed their organization to build a picture of the culture (more in Chapter 4) and assessed it as being highly centralized, averse to delegation, risk/failure intolerant and siloed. I asked how much they were prepared to change the way that they worked to enable agility; for example, adapting their processes and their governance. They said 'not so much' from which I concluded they should not waste money trying to be more widely agile as their current culture was toxic to agility. Privately I observed that they were building a commercial risk, as disruptors in their industry were likely to take market share but this was not the question I was asked to address.

So much for organizational agility. I also said that agility can be applied to aspects of an organization's operations, returning considerable value. By way of example, the Standish Group's 2018 Chaos Report,[4] a comparison of project success rates, revealed:

- 42% of projects using an agile approach were successful;
- 23% of projects using a waterfall approach were successful.

On that basis the verdict is clear: agile projects are more successful than waterfall projects.

A word of caution about the Standish and similar surveys. Are they really asking about agility in relation to projects of software development or about project management? In Chapter 3 I will show why this is an important distinction.

I conclude then that not only is the value case for becoming agile made. But that many organizations dare not delay becoming agile. And yet they persist in ways of working that may destroy them over the medium term, because their short-term adherence to what's familiar and comfortable is too powerful.

The Agile Manifesto – the foundation of agile

In *The Lord of the Rings*, Bilbo the hobbit volunteers to take the One Ring to Mordor and cast it into the fire to destroy the evil Sauron – because he feels responsible as the one who started 'this business'. Gandalf the wizard reminds him that when he found the ring it was only a part of its journey. He did not create the ring. Fortunately, better heads prevail and it is Bilbo's nephew Frodo who offers to take up the baton… the ring.

The Agile Manifesto did not create the problem. My own road to agile started in 1987 and I recognize some agile behaviours in a project way back then.

The group of highly experienced software developers who defined the Manifesto principles provided a huge marker on the road to agile. They are so influential that to build and describe agile project management (which we will do in Chapters 5–8), we must first understand and then adapt the Manifesto.

The Agile Manifesto consists of 12 **principles** and four **values**.

A reminder, these are just principles. They are not sacred. They are not written in stone on a high hill, nor are they entirely scientific and so are open to interpretation. They do however fundamentally help shape how we try to work in an agile way.

The 12 principles in the Agile Manifesto are:

- *Our highest priority is to satisfy the customer through early and continuous delivery of valuable software.*

I.e., focus on delivering value. Do the most valuable stuff first; 'fail fast' is a term often used by agile developers to mean that if you are going to fail, it's best this is known as early as possible.

- *Welcome changing requirements, even late in development. Agile processes harness change for the customer's competitive advantage.*

I.e., be flexible to maximize customer value. Responding to change is more important than sticking to a plan.

- *Deliver working software frequently, from a couple of weeks to a couple of months, with a preference for the shorter timescale.*

I.e., a) the quicker value can be delivered the better, b) there is less time for something to go wrong, and, c) for external factors to severely impact delivery.

- *Business people and developers must work together daily throughout the project.*

In a waterfall development, business people, such as subject matter experts (SMEs), users, tend to be involved only at certain points in the life-cycle (e.g. requirement specification and user acceptance testing). Under agile software development, it is critical for the development team to be together continuously across the development life-cycle. This level of engagement means that a) good decisions can be quickly made and b) there is less risk of misunderstanding, among other positives.

- *Build projects around motivated individuals. Give them the environment and support they need, and trust them to get the job done.*

People work best when they understand and feel good about what they are doing. Make it easy for them to work well, removing barriers, or simply not putting them in the way. Anything from ensuring they have promised resources and/or a pleasant workspace. Ensuring they do not have to spend half their lunch break travelling to buy a sandwich. If they know what to do, have the needed capability and feel good, then why not let them get on with it?

- *The most efficient and effective method of conveying information to and within a development team is face-to-face conversation.*

Communicate, communicate, communicate.

- *Working software is the primary measure of progress.*

Regular outputs that provably work and do what they should.

- *Agile processes promote sustainable development. The sponsors, developers and users should be able to maintain a constant pace indefinitely.*

Do create an environment that challenges both individuals and teams to stretch and challenge themselves. Do not create an environment which pushes so hard that people/teams burn out.

- *Continuous attention to technical excellence and good design enhances agility.*

Agile is not an excuse for cutting corners. Maintaining technical excellence, e.g. coding standards, is important to ensure testing is easier if there is consistency and the product is easier to maintain.

- *Simplicity, the art of maximizing the amount of work not done, is essential.*

Once you have an output that works (meets the stated need), STOP. I.e. do just enough.

- *The best architectures, requirements and designs emerge from self-organizing teams.*

If you have the right people in the team, who can produce what is needed, they will be highly self-motivated to do so. It is often more difficult to stop the creative process (see previous principle).

- *At regular intervals, the team reflects on how to become more effective, then tunes and adjusts its behaviour accordingly.*

A self-sustaining cycle of learning and improving is highly beneficial. Just ask any elite sports person. This becomes a built-in agile behaviour where the team regularly challenges itself.

In addition to its principles, the Agile Manifesto also reflects four **values**. Note that these are intended for software development and were not defined with project management in mind.

- *Individuals and interactions over process and tools*

Agile places more importance on people over process and even tools. People respond to business needs and drive the development process. Process and tools play an important supporting role to flexible, collaborative behaviours, which are more responsive to change to meet customer needs.

- *Working software over comprehensive documentation*

Documentation should not drive development, but be an output from it that is usually required and not left out. The level of detail and how approvals are done should be as streamlined as possible. While documentation has its value, in the agile mindset, it is software that is paramount. This is one area where intelligent use of automated processes can be highly efficient.

- *Customer collaboration over contract negotiation*

The collaborative agile team includes all parties: customers, delivery specialists etc. Therefore, the focus is constantly on customer needs. Collaborative behaviours also mean that all parties in the team have a win-win mindset, towards a common main goal. Contracts can reflect this more straightforward way of working.

- *Responding to changes over following a plan*

While change happens, it's to be avoided as much as possible when working in a traditional project management methodology. With agility, the key is to assess changes that will add value. However, agile development usually works in short iterations, sometimes called sprints. Their brevity allows for changes, even embracing them as a way to improve a development and add value.

Adapting the Agile Manifesto to projects

Let me turn things around a bit here and address the **values** of project agility first. When these values are adapted to project management, the changes are subtle, although the effects are not.

- *Individuals and interactions over process and tools*

It is people that deliver projects, not processes or tools. Agility places at least as much importance on people over process/tools. Therefore, how projects are run and governed, at both project and organizational level, must view people, their behaviours, relationships, needs and so on, with as much seriousness as process. Not forgetting that projects have to work within an organizational landscape, which usually includes some mandatory governance and assurance aspects. In practice, the people/process/tools aspects must be integrated and balanced.

- *Working outcomes over comprehensive documentation*

Projects are about producing outcomes which, when exploited, deliver benefits, i.e. value. That is what projects are for. Being agile means keeping things simple and avoiding unnecessary work. For example, documentation can be optimized to just what is needed – just enough, produced and delivered in the simplest way. This allows the team to focus on the outputs and their outcomes.

- *Customer collaboration over contract negotiation*

The same as for software development. The collaborative agile team includes all parties: customers, delivery specialists and so on. Therefore, customer needs are continually focused on. Collaborative behaviours also mean that all parties in the team have a win-win mindset. Contracts can reflect this more straightforward way of working.

- *Responding to changes over following a plan*

This for many is the most challenging agile value. A project swims in one direction. Too free an attitude to change risks fragmenting the project and wrecking value delivery. Under agile project management, change should be welcomed, but only if the change enhances or at least maintains the value delivered. Streamlined change control is crucial, which means you need to weed out early any change which does not clearly enhance benefits (more on this under change control later). Another difference is that agile software development assumes iterative development; in other words, in chunks or sprints (as opposed to phases. The big difference it that a sprint delivers a useable element, rather than just part of work-in-progress). An agile project can have ANY life-cycle, and a programme may contain many.

A generic life-cycle can be seen in Figure 1.2 below.

Figure 1.2: Generic project life-cycle

Having adapted the four Agile Manifesto values for project management, now let's turn to a view of how the 12 principles can be adapted to projects.

Principles of agile project management

These principles drive the mindset of teams and individuals, from the project to the executive. Given that projects exist to deliver value/benefits, this is where we will start.

- *Focus on delivering value*

Few people today would argue that the purpose of any project or programme is to deliver value. However, it should be said that even 15 and certainly 20–25 years ago most project management training focused on the purpose of projects as being to produce outcomes. Other people worried about whether those outcomes were producing benefits.

This was because projects delivered their outcomes, their assets or their capabilities and then closed. The capability produced was then put into use and then hopefully value was derived from it in some form. By this time the project was usually over and the team moved on.

Think about it. How many IT projects ended when the system was handed over to the client and how many construction projects closed with handover? In both these examples, the reality is that the value of the investment depends *entirely* on what the users of the software or the inhabitants of the building do with what has been delivered to them.

'Not my problem.'

Today, however, the purpose of any project is to deliver capability in order to derive benefits.

Agile project management is no different in this respect. What is different is the mindset of an agile project team in that the team focuses continually on the project's end goals. Everything the team does – the way in which they work, how they deal with change, how they prioritize work – must always be tested against the question: *is this going to maximize value from this project?*

Which means, of course, that the project must be very clear about its goals and outcomes from the start and they must be measurable, whether directly or indirectly. Justification for a project, i.e. the value to be gained, will usually be expressed in a business case.

If you have read about agile software development, you may have come across the term *minimum viable product* (MVP). In agile project management this represents the minimum outcomes required to make the project worth doing. If more can be delivered with the time and money available, so much the better.

N.B. Project outcomes are not always financial, especially in the public realm, e.g. reducing homelessness. Be mindful about how you will define what viable means for any project.

To allow focus on the MVP while delivering more scope if possible, prioritization of requirements at the outset of a project is critical.

- *Satisfy the customer*

Being customer focused is very much a sign and the commercial mantra of our times. Agile project management is no different. I have separated it from focus on delivering value because projects and especially programmes have stakeholders. Some will be customers for whom the value is being delivered. Other stakeholders may be impacted by the project, such as householders living near the proposed route of HS2.

Assessing satisfaction is mostly via project controls which show progress. Agility requires that to be openly, provably done, i.e. tell me *and* show me. Irrespective of life-cycle, a project must be able to demonstrate regular real progress. Even if it is only: here is this bit, it works, look… OK… next! There should be an audit trail from goal to proven output.

Satisfying the customer also means that there should be regular open and honest communication, even if progress news is not good, in order to gain and maintain trust.

Part of gaining trust is the ability to show that the agile project is under control. Some writers on agile play down or even seem to ignore the need for any project assurance. Agile has never meant no documentation or no control, only optimizing the level of control. And I prefer the word optimized rather than minimize because minimizing project assurance in agile project assurance can strongly imply leaving out something that is needed.

All the while show that the focus of project management is on leading delivery and that control aspects are not getting in the way.

- *Clear roles and responsibilities*

In 'traditional' project management it is important for there to be clarity over the roles and responsibilities for all involved in and related to a project. While being agile in projects is essentially the same, agility also encourages flexibility. If necessary and perhaps for short periods of time, role flexibility can be beneficial. For example, when a team member is away on holiday and another team member can step into their role temporarily, then that is being flexible – that is agility.

Agility also requires commitment from senior roles, especially the sponsor, to a high degree of engagement with their project.

- *Do just enough*

Just enough is at the heart of agility. A project needs to be literally just good enough in all of its respects. For some this carries connotations of not good enough but from a qualitative quality management sense just good enough literally means good enough but no more.

There should be no additional benefit in making an output, an outcome or capability from the project any better than it needs to be to suit its purpose. In fact, that will almost certainly take more time and cost more money and probably tie up key resources for longer than needed. And it will deny resources to other, perhaps operational, activities or other projects.

Finding out what just enough looks like is the tricky part and more on that in Chapter 4. In general, if the requirements and acceptance criteria are developed enough to build a business case, that should carry through to design and build. Another reason why the audit trail is important – so that you can always go back and check, and prove the solution meets requirements.

For the management aspects of the project, it must be visibly under control and be compliant with appropriate organizational governance. However, agility means challenging what you are doing. Do we really need this report, this level of detail, this meeting?

- *Embrace changing requirements*

This is one of the most difficult aspects of agility for projects, as mentioned earlier. Traditionally change within a project is often fought against and rejected as far as possible.

Being agile means being more open to change during a project, but remembering the focus on value. Any proposed change must enhance the value being delivered or at least maintain it.

- *Supportive environment*

Kotter, the change management guru, promotes very strongly the establishment of the energy for change and then sustaining that energy.

Being agile means that projects need to be able to flourish, to thrive within their organizational landscape. In many organizations projects do not fit very easily nor work very well with operational (business as usual) processes and procedures. Projects also often struggle to gain and maintain resources, or the attention of key stakeholders, within the customer organization.

This has always been and remains a key challenge for any project, programme or portfolio. But for agile project working to succeed, having a sustained supportive project landscape is critical.

This also applies inside a project. Again, this is not new; programme management evolved in part to provide an umbrella under which its projects can thrive.

- *Empower the team*

Organizations often claim to empower teams and individuals. But this is much more difficult to demonstrate.

Agility means that the project is empowered properly by its governance landscape and it also means that the project leadership both delegates authority and encourages individuals and teams within the project to act on that authority. It is also about creating an atmosphere in which people feel they are able to speak up to make suggestions, be creative or challenge. They feel that they can take decisions rather than sticking their heads above the parapet waiting to have them shot off.

- *Collaborative behaviours*

Collaborative behaviours are another aspect at the heart of being agile.

Earlier I stated this means that all parties involved support a win-win relationship. This requires openness about what each party needs to achieve to gain reasonable benefit from the project. Especially with customer–supplier relationships.

Collaboration must be built into every aspect of how a project will operate, from its procedures and working behaviours, to schedules in contracts between a client and supplier organization. N.B. Collaboration does not mean that everyone gets involved in everything.

Can agility survive if parts of a team do not work collaboratively? Chapter 4 will explore that complicated issue.

- *Reflect, learn and adjust*

Project reviews have traditionally included learning lessons from a completed project, and even during a project. The introduction of stage gates formalized lesson learning. But all too often lessons tend to be recorded but not used. Hell is paved with good intentions (Samuel Johnson).

Agility suggests two levels of actions to make this work. Agile project teams work closely together, sparking off each other and there is openness both to sharing an idea or lesson, and to receiving them. 'Someone might just have a better way of doing this than me…'. At the organizational level, perhaps led by an enterprise PMO, there's a mechanism for capturing and sharing learnings. But the learning culture also needs to be developed.

- *Fail early*

A common traditional project behaviour, not unreasonably, is to want to demonstrate progress early on. Senior management like 'quick wins' or 'low-hanging fruit'. These are often chosen to deliver first because they are quick and easy.

The fallacy here is that these early outputs may not be of particular value or priority to the customer and disguise much greater difficulty later on. Yes, agility promotes delivery and often, but not just anything to show progress. Being agile (agility) means having a focus on value. Which means that a project should choose a path that provides the greatest chance of delivering the most value. This is done in two ways:

1. By delivering the highest-priority outcomes first if practical, such as being subject to dependencies.
2. By addressing the highest risks early. The idea being that you do the difficult stuff first and the rest should be easier, more certain. Plus, if the project proves undeliverable, e.g. a viable solution cannot be found, it is better to discover that early, saving costs, time and embarrassment.

Chapter 2

Setting the scene for project agility

This chapter sets the scene for the descriptions of project agility and how to build it, which will come in the following chapters.

Lean vs. agile

Lean and agile are terms that are often used interchangeably, which just adds to the confusion around agility. Sometimes they are even used together – a dead giveaway that someone is not being clear.

While there are many commonalties between the two, I find it useful to think of lean and agile in different contexts.

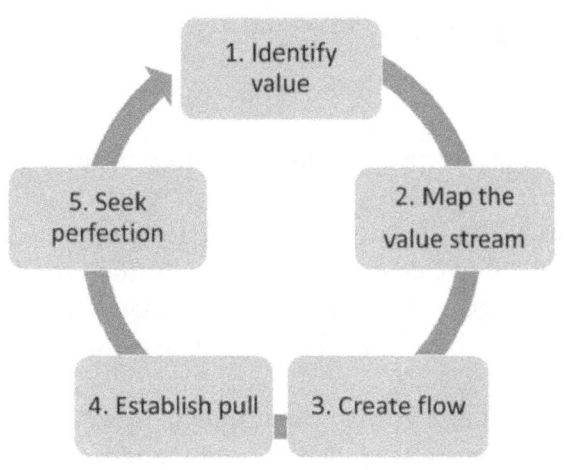

Figure 2.1: Lean process flow

Although arguably much older, lean is commonly recognized as a by-product of the Japanese automotive industry, notably Toyota, in the later 1940s. It emerged as a continuous process for the improvement of the production line. The lean approach is shown in Figure 2.1.

Lean consists of five processes applied in a continuous loop, whereas agile has emerged largely from software development that tends to be done in finite chunks, often in projects which of course have a start and finish. It makes sense then to reserve lean for continuous process and agile for project-based activity, as a rule of thumb.

- Use lean for continuous process, e.g. a production line.
- Use agile for finite process, e.g. project activity.

If you want to read more about a comparison of lean vs. agile, see the appendix.

People, Process and Tools

Principles are all very well but they only become useful when they are applied in practice. Chapters 5–8 will explore what the components of project management look like when agility is applied, such as scheduling, risk and stakeholder management and leadership. To be coherent, these components need to be brought together into a framework, as they are in APM's *Body of Knowledge* or PRINCE2. Something that adapts current best practice to show how things look with agility applied.

The cornerstones of the framework for project agility are provided by the interaction of *People*, *Process* and *Tools*.

People

Since I started my own project management journey in 1986, the evolution of the profession has been a joy both to watch and be a part of.

Once I moved from systems analyst to project manager, I was trained in something called PROMPT, which stood for *Project Resource Organization Management and Planning Techniques*. It was popular in government projects and the then still public sector organizations like British Telecom.

PROMPT influenced the subsequent process frameworks of PRINCE (Projects in a Controlled Environment) and then PRINCE2.

As the acronyms and their expanded titles indicate, these concepts drew on a view of project management as highly mechanistic; one that gave little importance to the role of people and behaviour. It is often said that people, especially how they behave and interact, is at the heart of being agile.

Much has changed in the profession to pave the way for agility in projects. In the 1990s the ever-increasing amount of transformation project-based activity, and especially its size and complexity, led to the conclusion that existing project management methods were not suited to managing it. New forms evolved in the form of programme and then portfolio management.

These were still mostly mechanistic, focusing on process excellence. But a race car is only as good as its driver. How people and teams behaved was increasingly recognized as important factors in success or failure. And so people factors drove the addition of techniques such as leadership, team building and communication into bodies of knowledge and methods.

These started to build a seed bed within which agility could then take root.

The iron triangle, coined by Dr Martin Barnes in 1969, has been with us for more than 50 years and remains a central idea. *All* projects can be defined by it.

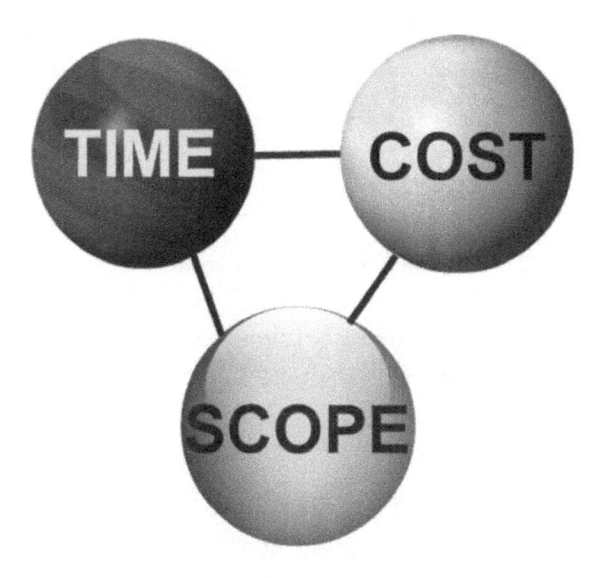

Figure 2.2: The iron triangle

The model is very rooted in a view of projects as static processes, with fixed requirements and ending with an output. Today's view of projects is considerably more nuanced and recognizes that 'the controlled environment' referenced in PRINCE is rarely, if ever, achievable; at least not if you want to deliver something that doesn't risk redundancy before completion.

Adapting agility to projects encourages a fresh look at the iron triangle. Is there another factor which defines and constrains *any* project? I believe the answer is yes and the factor is people.

How people behave, interact and organize is a factor which should be assessed and its constraints defined for any project. Every bit as much as the timescale, quality/scope or cost.

The iron triangle remains valid but it should now become the iron pyramid, or rather, the iron tetrahedron.

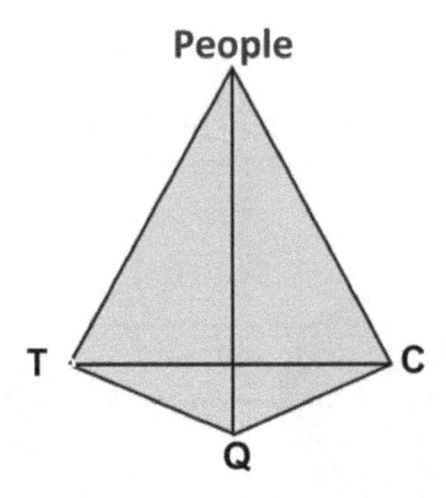

Figure 2.3: The iron pyramid

People as an integral part of being agile is a key differentiator for agile project management from other adaptations.

Process

About 20 years ago I spoke at a conference of PRINCE2 project managers. I made what I thought was a harmless and, to me, obvious remark that PRINCE2 was more a toolbox to be adapted than a cookbook to be followed. In the furore that ensued I thought I might be burned at the stake as a heretic. Most of that audience clearly believed PRINCE2 was a recipe to be followed quite strictly.

Since then, I have watched with pleasure the growth of the framework. Detailed project management methods such as those described in PRINCE2, the Association for Project Management (APM) and Project Management Institute (PMI) Bodies of Knowledge (BoKs) are very important. They provide a consistency to the understanding of risk management, planning, reporting and other project techniques, forming the knowledge base for any project professional.

Frameworks, as the name suggests, provide the basic structure. Thus, a requirement to 'have a plan' does not prescribe how that plan should be built or implemented. The nature of the plan is largely left up to the project manager to interpret according to the needs of their project. Frameworks may be based on a particular method, for example, PRINCE2, Managing Successful Programmes (MSP) and so on. But they don't provide a detailed blueprint. Instead, they concentrate on, for example, how change control should work in a particular organization, rather than the specifics of what form those controls will take. In other words, frameworks enable organizations to adapt project management methods to their needs and environment.

Tools

Younger readers may find it difficult to believe, but there was a time when we project managers, working remotely, perhaps in a hotel, struggled to connect using a standard phone line and a 56kbps modem, to send and receive project information. Processing speeds along with internet speed and bandwidth have all grown incredibly.

While technology increasingly assists the project professional, I should offer a couple of words of warning:

Firstly, I have long maintained that tools serve the processes and the people who operate them.

Any toolset needs to be configured to how the organization currently works, or is intended to work if change is a significant feature in the project. It is rarely wise to invest in expensive tools – and their expensive configuration – until you have established some maturity and stability in processes, report templates and so on. This too is an expression of agility. It encourages a 'just enough, but no more' approach to configuration.

👍 Maturity of process before tool.

Another word of caution is about the seductiveness of IT.

Take artificial intelligence (AI), for example. AI is currently of great interest and rightly so. In our profession the question *can AI replace project managers?* is being seriously asked, and seriously considered.

However, as Dr Ashley McNeile put it to me: 'AI for managing people in projects would require a huge data set of complex behaviours and interactions, many of which are not fully understood or lend themselves to be represented as meaningful data. So do not hold your breath.'

In the meantime, I look forward to technology and streamlined processes allowing project managers more time to do that most important of functions, managing other people.

Project and organization

Figure 2.4: A project's landscape

Project success is dependent both on what happens inside the project and what is going on in the surrounding landscape. Most project management methods and frameworks are concerned with looking inwards into the project and overlook the changes that may be occurring in the hinterland.

Even with the move towards flat organizations and reduced silo working, the basic challenge remains. How can we accommodate a project? Projects are temporary, cross-functional, even cross-departmental, demanding of operational resource. They do not fit neatly alongside business-as-usual activities and yet they compete with them.

In many organizations, projects have a similar status to viruses in the human body, eliciting the equivalent of an immune response to restrain or even kill what is seen as alien or non-conforming. This is an autonomic response rather than necessarily a conscious one.

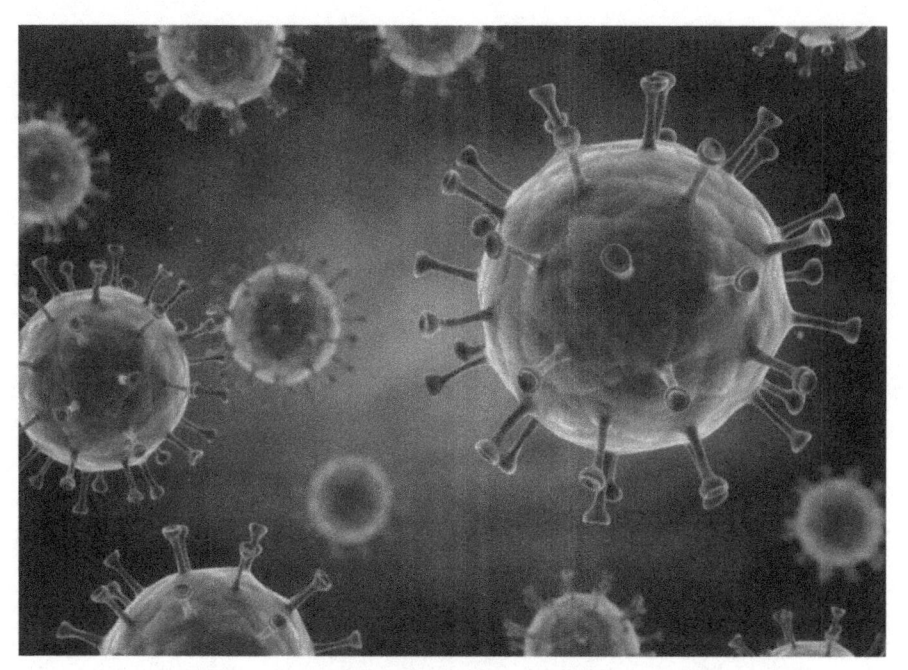

Figure 2.5: Project as a virus in an organization's body

Imagine this conversation which, while paraphrased, is a real example.

Project manager: Amanda the sales director suggested I come and talk to you. I need some help configuring the new CRM system we are buying and some of the experienced salespeople from your team are ideal to help us get things right.

Sales manager: I will see what I can do. We are stretched at the moment but I might be able to let you have someone a day or so a week for a short while.

Project manager: They do need to be experienced; someone who understands how sales works in detail and be able to suggest improvements. And I will need them full time.

Sales manager: They? And my best people? For long?

Project manager: Only four to five months

Sales manager: Months!? That will take us into the summer, which is when we struggle to maintain customer engagement with the holidays. No way can I let you have more than one and not for that long. My team has sales targets to hit for their bonus. Any I lend you will lose that for a start and they won't be happy.

Project manager: The new system will enable more sales to be made.

Sales manager: In the meantime, my team don't get their bonus, I get carpeted for missing sales targets and I may lose my best people who haven't made a bonus. How can you help me?

Sadly, this is a lose-lose situation. If the sales manager seconds key resources, their team performance will suffer and people will miss their bonus. Plus, of course, the organization may generate less revenue and possibly even harm customer relations. On the other hand, if the project manager does not get the expert resource he or she needs, their project could fail. There needs be a way to change this to win-win for them and the company.

Other common risks from the hinterland include:

- Sponsors who are too busy with their day job to fulfil their project role.
- Governance which is designed for business-as-usual operations not these pesky projects.
- Funding confusion: where is the budget coming from? Especially if there are multiple operational stakeholders.
- Cost tracking. I have seen projects spend mis-allocated across up to five ledgers for a complicated cross-functional programme,

requiring huge effort each month to track down and transfer costs to the correct programme cost centre.
- Tracking internal costs. Where most working is in silos, a project is working across silos and internal transfer charging is being used, this again becomes costly project administration with no net value to the project or organization.
- Access to shared services, e.g. finance, HR, audit, internal communications, procurement.

All these and more are not issues for business-as-usual operations as that is what they are set up to support. Any framework for project agility will therefore also need to include what happens in the organizational hinterland. More on this in Chapters 2 and 7.

How far should an organization go to accommodate projects?

The key question. Is it worth investing in an organization that allows projects to *thrive*?

It's a compelling question as it may not be worthwhile for your organization to invest significantly in building a project delivery capability, i.e. you simply do not do enough project-based activity to make the investment viable. More on this in Chapter 9.

There is nothing wrong with 'traditional' project management

Adrian Dooley, among others, rightly observes that 'traditional project management' is often used pejoratively, especially by some agilists: where the traditional means bureaucratic, rigid and slow. PRINCE2 is often cited as the epitome of tradition, documentation and process heavy. This puzzles me as I have adapted PRINCE2 for many clients needing to be compliant with UK government standards, in ways that agilists would recognize.

The project management is not the issue; how you use and adapt it is the key. The less experienced may be more inclined to follow a recipe, to document more to be *on the safe side*. Professionals have learned to adapt and not do more management than is needed. What better reflection of agility could you find?

When I use the term traditional, it is recognizing behavioural traits where the project management toolbox is not being used as effectively as it could be. Or that there is a culture or mindset that requires more bureaucracy in an organization.

Chapter 3

The five most dangerous assumptions about project agility

When an organization adopts agility, it is a major change and undertaking. It is critical to ensure that both those leading the change and those implementing project agility understand:

- what project agility is;
- what project agility is not;
- what might look like project agility but isn't and must be avoided.

I have worked with clients and have spoken with executives who simply will not have the word 'agile' mentioned. Some squirm with embarrassment when they reluctantly admit their organization's fingers have been burned from getting project agility badly wrong. Sometimes agile itself gets the blame, and I am sorry to say that a bad worker does sometimes blame their tools.

Then there are the multitude of colleagues with whom I have discussed agility in projects. As often happens in the company of peers, we share 'war stories'. Of course, as professionals we do this to learn and grow, but we also do it as we are getting a little older and like to complain to each other.

Out of these discussions and anecdotes I have distilled the following top five most expensive and dangerous assumptions and misunderstandings arising from so-called 'agile project management'.

The top five mistakes in implementing agile:

- Scrum is project management.
- Agile projects must be iterative.
- Agile means leaving stuff out.
- C level does not 'get' agility.
- Senior management is insufficiently engaged.

Scrum isn't project management

Even if you have no exposure to software development but have googled agile or agile project management, it is highly likely that you will have encountered Scrum. It is one of the most common software development frameworks that has grown out of (or with, depending on your view of history) the Agile Manifesto. If you have not come across it but are looking into agility, then you certainly will encounter Scrum.

This huge mistake comes in as the clear number 1. Web search agile project management and much of the material you will find will conflate project management with software development. They are *not* the same. Now I started my project career in IT (enabled) projects and the historic close relationship between project management and software development is obvious. The mistake is trying to use Scrum, or any software development framework, *instead* of project management.

Essentially, Scrum promotes breaking up software development into bite-sized chunks, each of which can be built in a series of iterations – short development life-cycles, typically two weeks long. Once integrated, these separately developed chunks should form the desired software outcome.

Figure 3.1 shows a typical Scrum diagram. Note its components. It starts with a list of requirements and a Scrum team. It finishes when that team has delivered as much of those requirements as practical in the form of working software.

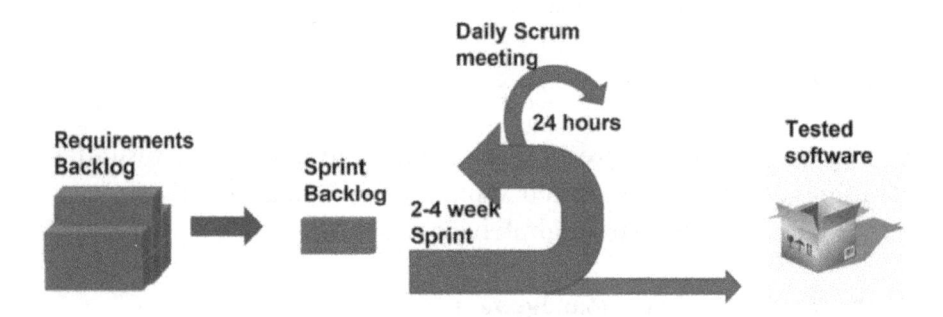

Figure 3.1: A typical Scrum diagram

Many would say and have said that sounds like a project. There is a finite time, scope and set of resources. It meets the triple project characteristics for a project: time/cost/scope(quality).

And so the foundations for confusion are laid.

Now look at Figure 3.2.

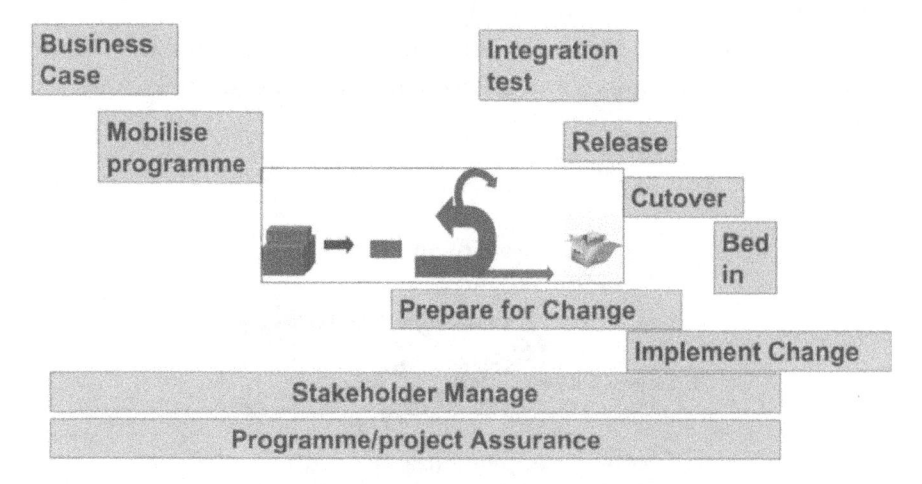

Figure 3.2: An IT-enabled project containing scrum

Superficially, at a distance, in a poor light on a wet and rainy night, Scrum might look like project management. But there is a great deal more to a project than what Scrum does. Ask yourself even these few questions:

- Where did the purpose come from and how was it defined?
- How is this work being funded, by whom and how was this achieved?
- How were the Scrum team resources obtained, especially the subject matter experts?
- How is the working software to be used, by whom and what preparation is needed?
- How will the working software be introduced into live operation and with what controls?
- Is this work dependent on anything else, or vice versa?
- How is this activity being controlled within the organization?

- What are the interests of external stakeholders and how are they going to be managed?
- How is this work going to prove its value?

The Scrum framework does not encompass any of the above and cannot address any of those questions. And yet, there are few projects where those questions do not apply.

Figure 3.3 shows a more realistic scope of what even the most basic project management does and it is well beyond what Scrum is designed to do.

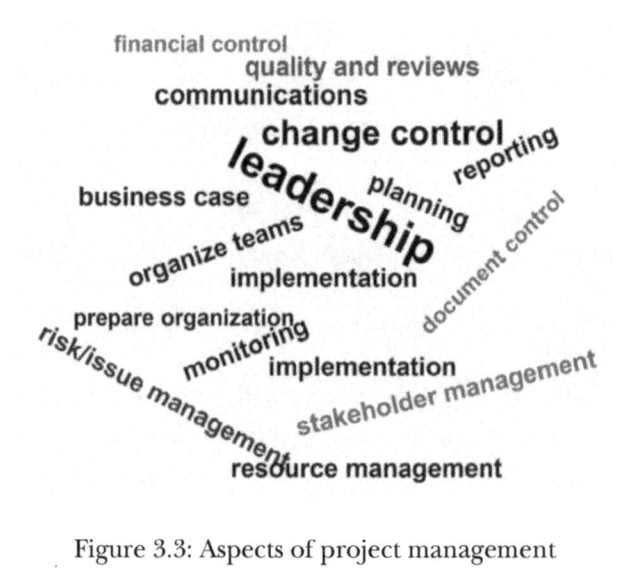

Figure 3.3: Aspects of project management

Any management framework or method must be capable of general applicability and adaptability.

Can you bend Scrum out of shape or add to it to make it look like project management? Yes of course but why would you? That is not adapting; it is hammering a nail into a wall using a rolling pin to hang your favourite picture in the vain hope it will stay there, instead of using a drill, screw, fixing and screw-driver. Adapting is one thing; using completely the wrong tool is quite another.

Agile projects must be iterative

The second most likely information you will find if you web search agile project management will inform you that agile projects have iterative life-cycles. Which must mean that *only* projects with iterative life-cycles can be managed with agility. This is nonsense and incredibly limiting for two reasons.

Firstly, it makes no sense to have an approach that is limited to just one type of life-cycle. Anyone who has had even limited exposure to projects and programmes is likely to have seen a number of life-cycles. Or at least variations on the generic life-cycle I showed in Chapter 1 and is repeated in Figure 3.4.

Figure 3.4: Generic project life-cycle

Notice how it proceeds from left to right in serial fashion, sometimes called *waterfall* as it flows in one direction from start to finish.

Now recall the Scrum development life-cycle, which is a series of iterations. But even this example sat within a project with an overall waterfall life-cycle.

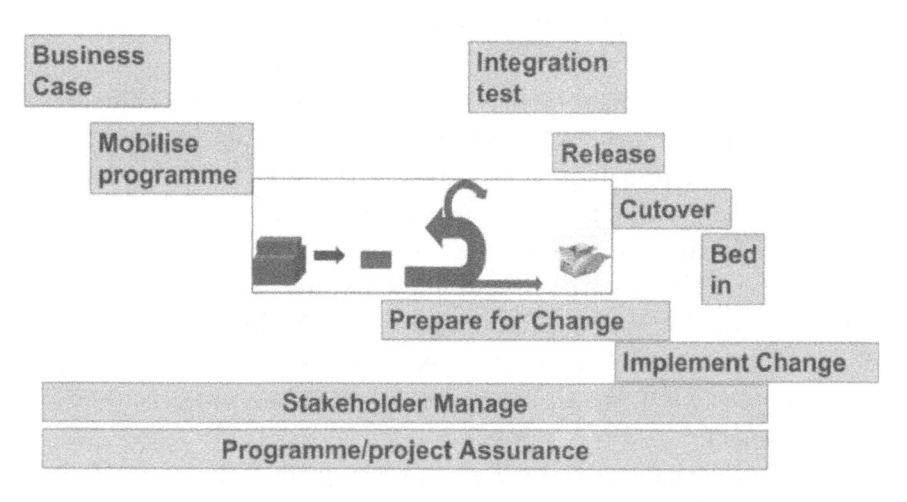

Figure 3.5: An IT-enabled project containing scrum

Or how about a programme of projects where there also may be multiple phases such as shown in Figure 3.6. Here a commercial housing project is phased so that the income from initial phases can help fund later ones.

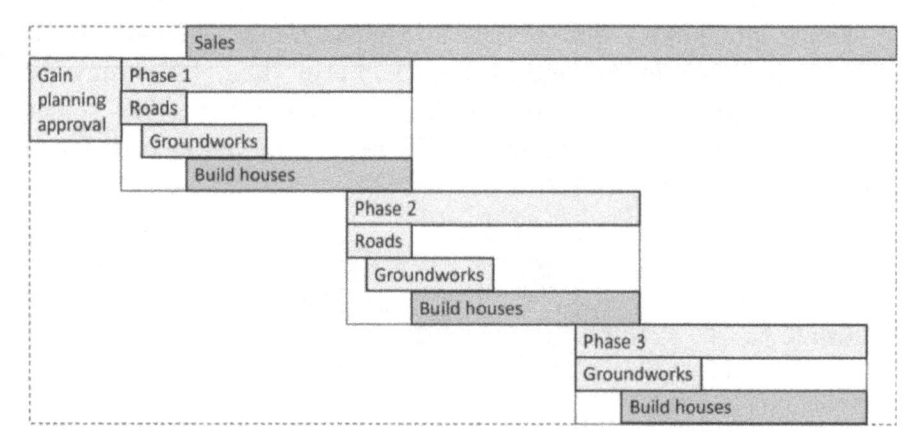

Figure 3.6: Commercial house build schedule

If project agility is to be useful it has to be generally applicable, not limited to only some types of projects. Imagine if you could only use a method for IT projects, or another bespoke one for engineering, or construction, or the public sector? Madness!

👍 An agile project or programme can have any appropriate life-cycle or combination of life-cycles.

Secondly, project management is about much more than a life-cycle. There are multiple processes such as change control, risk, and financial and document management. Also people aspects like leadership, stakeholder management and communications.

Another folly bred out of this is the non-debate over waterfall vs. agile projects. The debate of waterfall vs. iterative life-cycles is valid as you are comparing like with like. Unfortunately, the debate is usually mistaken to mean that if your project has a waterfall life-cycle, you cannot apply agility. Again, life-cycles do *not* define projects; they are just one aspect.

The notion that agility is *only* for projects with an iterative life-cycle is madness and plain wrong.

Agile means leaving stuff out

A short story to set the scene.

Stephen Carver of Cranfield University has a great story about a games producer trying to use agile, both to develop their games and to project manage their development. They called him up and asked his advice as they were having some challenges. On arrival the conversation went something like this:

Stephen: Describe for me your agile approach.

Director (looking both perplexed and hurt): What approach?

Stephen: Perhaps we can start with your agile development framework, is it Scrum for instance?

Director (now looking very confused): But we are agile (snapping his fingers and being very animated), we don't have an approach, we are free in how we work.

Stephen (with a professional sigh): Brew up lots of coffee, send out for sandwiches and muffins and let's make ourselves comfortable... this explanation is going to take a while.

A major selling point for agility is getting more from less. It is punchy and alluring to executives, especially finance ones. Unfortunately, that slogan has been twisted and debased into some dangerous and ultimately wastefully expensive interpretations. Here are some of the more common ones.

- You don't have to plan

This is alas quite appealing to quite of lot of people around projects. The tendency to get on with stuff is popular. The notion of working out what we want and how we are going to get it – as we go along – is not at all what the Agile Manifesto suggests and in the world of projects is anarchy.

If anything, being agile requires more discipline rather than less. A core behaviour is constant focus on the value being sought. Keeping an eye on the prize. Everything done on and during a project must be tested using the question: *is this the best way to get the most value?*

Being agile is about doing *just enough* planning, as will be discussed in Chapter 6.

- You don't need controls

As with planning, it is not that you do not need controls, but that you need just enough. In other words, do no more than you need to be in control or to be able to demonstrate it.

I have established portfolio, programme and project management capabilities for several major client organizations. A common complaint from project managers has been about reporting – whether its frequency or the level of detail. Sometimes I had to remind them that we needed to satisfy both their project assurance – what they need to do to be in control of their project – but also to adhere to the organization's governance. Sometimes that required reporting and other controls, beyond what was necessary for their needs. The challenge – and here is where agility came in – was to find an optimum overhead that would satisfy the needs of both project assurance and organizational governance.

More on this in Chapter 6.

- You don't have to do documentation

I started out designing and developing software in the old days of a computer language called COBOL and Job Control Language. At least I never had to use punch cards! I, along with most of my colleagues, hated doing documentation. We were sort of agile in that we tried to do the minimum design documentation to be able to get on with coding. Strange things called Data Flow Diagrams, Entity Models and Relational Data Analysis. Enough nostalgia, the point is, it was not until I joined a team maintaining a system that I longed for better documentation. Even worse, a colleague who is the System Design Authority for the replacement of a legacy system is losing sleep and his hair trying to trace documentation for a system that has 'evolved' over 20 years, mostly without any.

And consider how contractual issues would be addressed in a multi-supplier project where responsibilities are not clearly documented and where each party has their own clear idea of what is correct.

Sorry to belabour the point but being agile is about doing just enough. Whether that is documentation, planning, risk, stakeholder management, reporting and so on.

- You don't need business analysts

This is one up for debate.

Many agile development purists say you simply do not need business analysts as the agile development team contains both operational (e.g. subject matter experts, SMEs) and systems people, who work together all the time until the work is done. But I am not in favour of chucking the baby out with the bathwater.

- What if the project is not IT-enabled change? Who will help the SMEs and technical experts communicate with clarity?
- What if it is IT-enabled change but not using agile development methods? Again, who ensures clarity of requirements to solution design, acting as a translator between technical and non-technical people?
- Who can act as a moderator at the detail level?
- What if agile development methods are in use but immature?

There is a common theme here: the role of the business analyst in bridging the communications barrier between the SMEs/users and the technocrats.

In my experience I have mostly known two types of business analyst (BA): a business BA and a systems BA. Both roles are concerned with bridging the gap between the operational and the IT technical. The business BA is particularly skilled in bridging that gap, with the ability to translate the language of the operations people, users and subject matter experts (call them what you will) into the language and models, Epics and user stories of the systems analysts. *And* crucially, the other way around. The same is true with engineering, even marketing specialists, as specialists always have their own language. Think of the medieval guilds with their closely protected secrets.

A good BA is the magician gone rogue who can unlock and reveal the tricks of the trade.

N.B. It is common practice to call these business systems analysts, which for me just muddies the waters.

- You don't need project managers

I will not dwell on this one as the argument has been covered above under *Scrum isn't project management*. The false claim is that Scrum is a project management method. If that were true then a Scrum Master could fulfil the roles of a project manager. But Scrum is not project management and the role of Scrum Master is not that of a project manager.

Remembering this book is about being agile, i.e. agility in projects, it is worth noting that there is a circumstance where a project manager is not required. This is where the development activity simply does not need a project wrapper, agile or not. Two examples:

a) An investment finance business has product-based agile development teams. Each team comprises subject matter experts from the product team and IT developers. A Scrum framework is used to produce monthly updates on the product systems in the business. The product director is also the product owner in Scrum terms and the Scrum team is led by a Scrum Master. This is a business-as-usual process and a project wrapper would not add any value.
b) Small-scale developments, whether agile or not, where again a project wrapper would add no value.

A variation on b) could also be DevOps – which may or may not incorporate agile practice in the Dev bit.

C-suite does not 'get' agile

One the most persistent themes from my chats with colleagues is that many at the C-suite and executive level just do not 'get', i.e. understand, agility for projects. Even worse, commonly they do not 'get' projects at all.

If reading this you are in a senior role, this is not a criticism, but pretty much an inevitability. Most people running an organization are running a day-to-day operation. The roles are business as usual and in most organizations projects are not business as usual. People tend to be comfortable with the familiar. And uncomfortable, even fearful, with the unfamiliar.

This changes at the opposite end of the spectrum in organizations which are project based and therefore projects are the business as usual. Also in organizations that contain professional services, or other project-based groups, divisions or silos.

Lack of exposure to projects has two key consequences: *mindset* and *attention*.

Firstly, the mindset. Project thinking is different from business-as-usual thinking. Project people are generally *change* people. We like change; projects are mostly about change. Business as usual is about keeping the show on the road. Before you start shouting, I know that good business managers are always seeking to improve their operations. Yes, I get that and indeed wrote earlier about use of Lean for such. That is about continuous improvement, not significant change in finite time with specifically allocated resources, i.e. projects. Senior people who have had operational careers think differently from those with projects backgrounds. Lack of exposure to project-type activities often leads to poor decision making and sometimes to no decision making. As the following fictitious conversation between a project manager and director testifies.

Project manager: I need your help with the lack of a subject matter expert from marketing.

Director: Can't you resolve that?

Project manager: I agreed a loan arrangement with the line manager three months ago and checked each month, now they won't let me have them.

Director: Why are you only telling me now?

Project manager: It's been on the risk list in each report and was escalated as an action to you last week.

Director: I was busy; tell the line manager you have spoken to me.

Project manager: They know it's been escalated and feel they don't have to do anything as nobody but me has pushed them.

Director: Do you really need the expert?

Project manager: (expletive deleted). Yes, the project now has a day-by-day delay until I get the right person.

And as the old saying goes: 'How does a project become a year late? One day at a time…'

The second factor is attention. This tends to occur in two ways. We all tend to focus on the familiar. As an operational director or manager, it's natural to concentrate on the 'day job', especially when something goes wrong. A director at an airport rightly told me once that ops trumps projects. If the ground radar packs up and planes cannot safely land, take off or manoeuvre, the engineering director will not be in a project review meeting.

When it comes to agility in projects, this is even more of a challenge as agility requires a sustained level of engagement. Which brings me to the second manifestation: taking your eye off the ball. Kotter has long researched and written on the need for especially senior management to sustain the energy of major change (see Figure 3.7). Again, because projects are not 'in the blood', it is all too easy for senior people to become distracted from even critical projects.

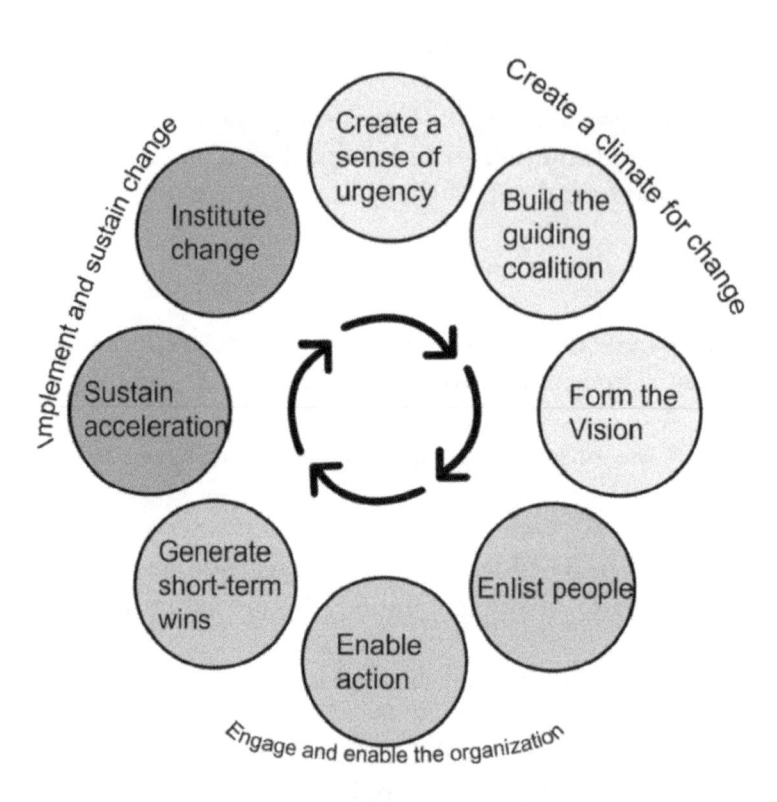

Figure 3.7: Kotter's eight-stage model for change

Senior management are insufficiently engaged

This mistake in part falls out of the previous one.

In 2015, the Association for Project Management published its *Conditions for Success* research report.[5] Twelve conditions were identified. Of those, three are directly related to senior management engagement:

- supportive organizations;
- capable sponsors;
- effective governance.

These findings have been strengthened by the recent follow-up report; *Dynamic Conditions for Project Success*.[6] The research report stated that its nine dynamic conditions are best achieved at the organizational level. A view also strongly expressed by the PMI's 2020 *Pulse of the Profession* report,[7] which stressed the importance of supportive organizations.

And now a short story. Several years ago, I was asked to help the executive team of a UK business school. They were having problems functioning as project sponsors. It soon became very clear that they well understood the role of sponsor – which is far from common. They simply did not have the time given their day-to-day roles.

It was not just a matter of not enough time. 'Project sponsor' was not actually in any of their job descriptions and their performance measures did not include project sponsorship. It was inevitable they would not make the time.

If projects are peripheral to 'core' operational activity, the ability and/or willingness to sustain their attention for projects is likely to be limited. Kotter's eight-stage change model remains valid and shows the risk to project success of the lack of sustained senior management engagement.

Chapter 4

Conditions for being agile

Projects frequently find themselves fighting for survival. Most organizations are based on operations comprising continuous business-as-usual processes (BAU), whereas projects and especially large change programmes are temporary. How BAU organizations function is often at odds with the needs of projects.

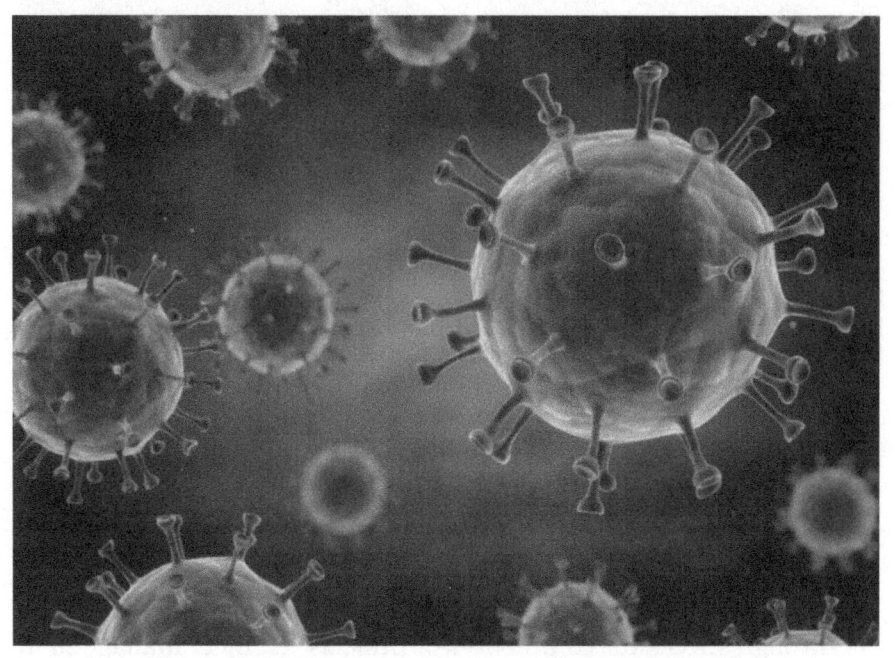

Figure 4.1: Project as a virus in the organization's body

Remember this from Chapter 2? This chapter is about the organizational landscape and how it needs to change so that agility can flourish.

Organizational culture – the project and agility killer – or enabler

In the Chapter 2 section *project and organization,* I discussed how project success or failure depends both on what happens inside a project and outside in its organizational hinterland. An idea of what this means is shown in Figure 4.2 below.

Figure 4.2: A project's landscape

    This hinterland is being increasingly recognized as important, especially given what I referred to in Chapter 2 as the *projectization of work,* and the rise of what is termed *project economy,* which is described by the PMI as: where 'people have the skills and capabilities they need to turn ideas into reality. It is where organizations deliver value to stakeholders through successful completion of projects' (Project Management Institute [PMI] website).

    To me the projectization of work is not new.

Example: British Telecom's (now called BT) Engineering Division 1992–1995
In the period I worked in their Engineering Division, all of the division's work was structured through projects, primarily as

the means of tracking work vs. spend against budget. There were two categories of project. Most were business as usual, such as laying cables, repairs and customer works. But some were transformation, mostly relating to major changes to the network, such as the move from electro-mechanical to digital exchanges, or the initial installation of the then new technology of fibre-optic cables.

A five-year business plan drove each annual business plan and budget, approximately £2bn per year. Each of the ten geographic regions bid for and was allocated part of this budget. Every penny was then allocated to BAU or Transformation, but always within projects. Each region would define BAU projects, e.g. for cable replacement, exchange maintenance and so on. Projects would run for the length of the financial year.

Since then, the projectization of work for BAU has grown considerably. Therefore, the importance of the project hinterland is becoming of critical importance as projects become a greater proportion of operations.

Both the PMI and the APM (Association for Project Management) have recognized that the organization impacts project success for good or ill. Later in this chapter I will examine what a landscape that is supportive of projects and agility can look like. To start I need to look at what drives project success or failure in that landscape, the *organizational culture*.

Organizational culture is the collection of values, policies, assumptions, practices, standards, structure, relationships and beliefs that inform and influence, often strongly, how people at all levels of an organization will behave. This is slightly different from the APM definition, which is limited to the unwritten rules that influence behaviour. Researchers like Edgar Schein have long suggested that the components of organizational culture are far broader than just assumptions people make. Schein's model has three components:

- Artefacts – tangible and visible elements that would be recognized even by those outside the culture, from branding to dress code.
- (Espoused) Values – an organization's stated values and rules, including from strategy to process.

- Assumptions – the often deeply embedded, taken-for-granted behaviours.

Example: A coffee company
With any new client I like to understand how the organization works and that is what I ask at the outset. The response I usually get consists of the company's vision, strategy, organization, policies, processes, systems, standards and so on. Which was all confirmed when I then spoke to the various operational groups. But I also discovered that it was far from the full picture.

The company had been highly successful in developing new business, and had grown its departments, i.e. sales, installation engineers, service department and so on. But the rapid growth had stretched to breaking point how they worked together. All sorts of work arounds were in place to keep pace with new business and service current customers, but not robustly. Causing frustration not just for customers, but in the workforce as well.

In the end, new and modified workflows, measurement and improved resource management solved most of the issues.

To help solve their problems I had to get under the surface.

I have found that organizational culture is like an iceberg (see Figure 4.3). Some of it is visible above the surface, e.g. vision, strategy and so on. But much more is out of sight and is where the APM definition is spot on.

In practice, *all* these components combine to define an organization's culture. And while that culture cannot determine how people act all of the time – people are way more complex than that – it does strongly influence how people behave on a day-to-day basis. It is also dangerous both for the Board and anyone brought in to run organizational change, since the culture they think they have may be quite wrong. Also remember the saying attributed to Drucker: 'culture eats strategy for breakfast'.

Having noted that warning, knowing that the components of culture can be identified and analysed means that if that culture needs to be changed/modified, then the levers that need to be pulled are understood.

Figure 4.3: The organizational culture iceberg

Organizational culture – the agility killer

In 2010–2011, in the aftermath of the last global financial crisis, I was invited separately by two UK-based financial institutions to discuss how they could take agility beyond their IT departments, where its use was successful.

A key part of my usual fact finding was to determine, in general, the culture of the organization through interviews and by reading what they wrote about themselves. E.g. their vision, strategy, governance policies and standards and so on. The evidence for both organizations were clear. They were quite risk averse, not surprising for financial organizations, especially in the wake of the financial crisis and several financial scandals. Neither organization had any involvement in those I hasten to add.

The key finding was that they were highly centralized and very reluctant to delegate significant authority in their business operations, let alone their business transformation activity.

Within their IT departments, agility was successful because it (at that time) was in effect ring-fenced. It was used within a scope of work largely under the control of IT and not generally used for IT-enabled business change activity.

My conclusion was then that their organizational culture was toxic to agility as:

- permitted delegations meant that only minor decisions could be taken locally;
- business-level teams could not be empowered sufficiently to be self-organizing;
- they were unwilling to change governance rules, processes and structures to support empowered projects;
- while they did appoint senior sponsors for business transformation projects, they were not able to engage sufficiently due to 'no room' being made for the role around their operational roles.

My advice was that unless they were willing to adapt their organizations to the needs of agility they should not go down that route. They did not, a tragic loss of significant consulting fees.

Organizational culture – when it enables projects to *thrive*

As individuals many of us look to role models. Professionals of all ages and levels have peers, coaches or mentors that help them to develop. Semi-retired as I am, there are still people I learn from. Some others have influenced me greatly, like Geoff Reiss, the great programme management innovator and guru, who is much missed.

So too can organizations learn from each other. If you want to know how your organization can become great at project value delivery, take a look at other organizations who are and what they do.

> **Key point:** A key common factor is that success is the result of a coherent and integrated approach comprising multiple factors.

Conditions for being agile 51

Example: Shell Project Academy

Shell, for example, have an integrated approach, much of which is summarized in Figure 4.4. It, and the Shell Project Academy in particular, grew out of a realization in the early 2000s, that project success rates could be greatly improved, and the solution was not simple. Shell's commitment continued even through the economic crisis in 2008 and continues.

Group	Component
People	
Organization	• Project visibility at Board level. • Four levels of project size/complexity. • Shell Project Academy (SPA) as basis of growing project competency globally. • Top professionals are rotated through SPA to pass on their expertise before returning to the field. • Collaboration with professional bodies, e.g. Association of Project Management.
Behaviour	• Development is both in the field and via the Shell Project Academy (SPA). • Career and personal development aligned to levels of project size/complexity. • Competency-based capability development. • Capability profiles reflect growing experience. • Capability profiles determine what level of project can be undertaken. • Very strong safety culture.
Process	• Business planning driven portfolio management. • Shell portfolio, programme and project management (P3) standards. • Technical standards for both Shell people and contractors.
Technology	• Corporate profile, programme and project management tools (e.g. dashboards, scheduling, risk, reporting).

Figure 4.4: A view of the Shell integrated project approach

The approach is well embedded. If you are familiar with maturity models, their maturity level is at least Level 4 with safety compliance and adherence to critical technical standards to Level 5. Nor does it stand still; a new competency toolkit was launched in 2018.

The results of this approach are high project success rates.

Neither Board nor senior management have much, if any, interest in the minutiae of project management, nor should they. They were interested in evidence that the integrated approaches would produce *value*. Because that, not project management jargon, is their language.

The conclusion has to be that if an organization modifies itself to allow projects to thrive – they will. These are the *supportive* organizations.

Therefore, the converse is also true if projects continue to have to fight for survival. Many will not and clearly operate in *non-supportive* organizations.

If you accept the former what does that mean? Surely all the components are already known:

- Project, programme and portfolio management.
- Software tools to support them, with interfaces to corporate management information tools, e.g. financial and corporate risk logs.
- Recognition of the value of collaborative working.
- Recognition of the importance of good leadership.
- Recognition of the value of effective, empowered teams.
- Governance standards and processes.
- Internal and external social media for communication channels...

I could go on...

What is less visible is how you pull these together, and how you sell that to the C-suite. Especially the CFO (Chief Financial Officer), who would love to have benefits at zero cost if they could.

Some years ago, I was working with colleagues Trevor Band and Brenda Hales with various clients. They posed the challenge of how to create *supportive* organizations in which projects can *thrive* and we called it *Organizational Project Management*.

Organizational project management and the project economy

The successful delivery of value by projects, programmes and portfolios is dependent both on what happens inside a project and in its organizational hinterland. Most project, programme and even portfolio management frameworks and guidance focus on projects and what happens inside them. This section considers the organizational hinterland.

Projects commonly either have to fight for attention, resources and so on, or they languish and even die, and there are three key reasons for this.

- Leadership commonly do not have backgrounds in projects.
- Financial, resourcing and other functions are not set up to support project activity.
- Operational management at all levels typically do not engage sufficiently with project activity.

Looking at these in turn, firstly, among FTSE 100 companies, few C-suite people have project-based careers. Instead, they tend to develop their careers within business-as-usual roles, e.g. financial management, marketing, legal, engineering and so on. That is, in keeping things going and growing the business rather than transformation and other project-based experience. Projects are not in their DNA.

Secondly, for most organizations strategic, business and financial planning are based on running and growing the business, through business-as-usual activities. Projects, especially in terms of transformation, are generally not a business-as-usual activity. Therefore, the governance and management structures are not set up to support them, but for business-as-usual, continuous operations. This makes projects feel like that shape in the child's puzzle for which there is no hole to match.

Thirdly, people involved in business-as-usual operations are busy, their time fully allocated to their operational functions. Then projects come along which certainly need a senior-level champion, the sponsor. They may well also need subject matter experts from the business, often the most experienced and knowledgeable. No line manager will easily or willingly give up their best people for months at a time to the potential damage of their departments and performance bonus.

These three reasons are evidenced by three things:

- 30 years of research into project success/failure factors, e.g. Standish Chaos, and professional body reports, which consistently include top ten factors both inside and outside of projects.
- Professional recognition, e.g. APM BoK 7 and PMI's Pulse of the Profession, both of which have long focused on best professional practice inside projects, but now write significantly of supportive organizational cultures. Such as the project economy.
- Looking at the characteristics of organizations that are good at doing projects.

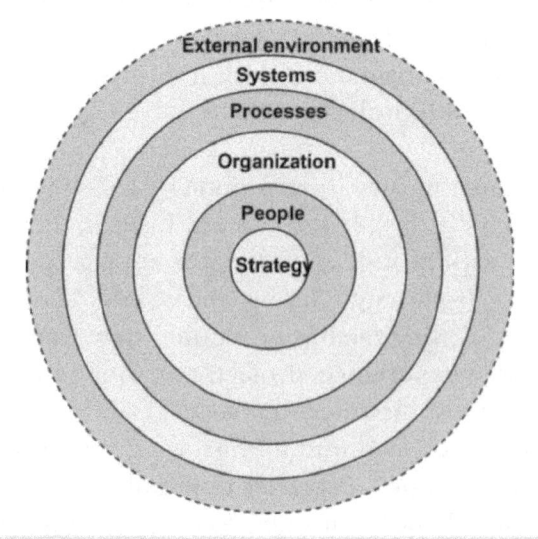

Strategy: Strategy includes both continuous (business-as-usual) and project activity.
People: The Board and all levels recognize the value of projects. Commitment is given to projects, with resourcing that enables sufficient levels of engagement where people have the space to work on projects as part of their day job. Facilitated by relationships between project and BAU leaders and shared service functions e.g. finance and HR.
Organization: Board-led commitment to behaviours that enable projects to thrive, without damaging business-as-usual activity. Engagement of resources to support projects, while maintaining the integrity of business-as-usual activity.
Processes: The organization's processes, e.g. governance, are adapted and developed to support effective value delivery by projects, alongside business-as-usual activity.
Systems: Information systems are adapted and developed to support both project and business-as-usual activity.
External environment: Projects visible as an integral part of the organization

Figure 4.5: Outline OrgPM Framework™

The OrgPMFramework™ is intended to describe a framework for organizational project management, which is *the creation of an organizational culture that enables projects to THRIVE*, and not merely survive or even die. It is very much a work in progress but its outline is shown in Figure 4.5.

The vision of the OrgPMFramework™ is that in all organizations with significant project-based activity, projects should be integral with business as usual.

Chapter 9 will expand on this framework, but some of its characteristics should include:

- Projects form part of the new operational business.
- Board 'gets' projects and agility.
- Board leads adoption of agility from the top.
- Delegation/autonomy down as far as possible – trusted teams.
- Governance modified to support project working.
- PM training part of all management training.
- Resourcing to fit the new BAU, not just to enable continuous processes but project working as well. E.g. assume subject matter experts will sometimes need to be backfilled when seconded to projects.
- Project exposure and working assumed part of anyone's career path.
- Projects a valid career path.

Avoiding the governance vs. assurance confusion

Agility seeks to avoid confusion through clarity and, where possible, through simplicity.

The terms governance and assurance are at once well defined and vague. Well defined in that there are lots of definitions, most of which are similar, which is good. Vague, as the terms are often used interchangeably. Here then is a suggestion which works for most of the definitions I have seen and, well, it works.

Assurance is about what you do *inside* a project/programme/portfolio to visibly reduce the risk of failure and increase the probability of success.

Governance is the framework of authority and accountability set by the organization(s) *outside* in the project hinterland.

Two quick examples.

a) A project needs funding. The organization's governance defines the need for a business case and the approval process.
b) During mobilization, the project manager defines the assurance approach to be used. This approach may include some mandatory aspects, e.g. must report a minimum defined dataset monthly into the owning organization. Here the organization's governance determines parts of the project's assurance.

Chapter 5

Adapting project management for agility – People

Setting the scene

Chapters 5 to 8 all deal with adapting agility to the whole range and scope of the project management profession. There is *much* more to project management agility than a life-cycle, iterative or otherwise. To avoid a huge unwieldy chapter I have divided up this main body of the book into:

    Chapter 5: Adapting project management for agility – People
    Chapter 6: Adapting project management for agility – Process
    Chapter 7: Adapting project management for agility – Tools and AI
    Chapter 8: Adapting project management for agility – Portfolios and programmes

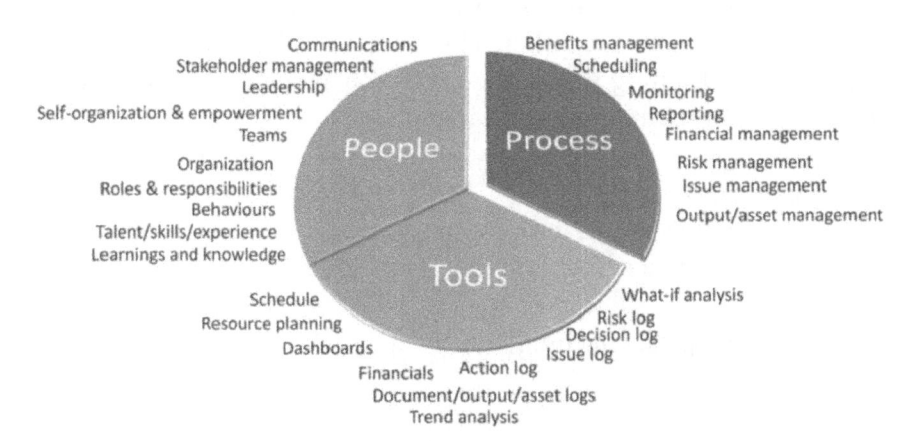

People
- Communications
- Stakeholder management
- Leadership
- Self-organization & empowerment
- Teams
- Organization
- Roles & responsibilities
- Behaviours
- Talent/skills/experience
- Learnings and knowledge

Process
- Benefits management
- Scheduling
- Monitoring
- Reporting
- Financial management
- Risk management
- Issue management
- Output/asset management

Tools
- Schedule
- Resource planning
- Dashboards
- Financials
- Action log
- Document/output/asset logs
- Trend analysis
- What-if analysis
- Risk log
- Decision log
- Issue log

Figure 5.1: People, Process, Tools model

Several years ago, the Association for Project Management (APM) held a workshop of invited attendees. The workshop examined the

APM's *Body of Knowledge* (BoK 6 at the time) and competencies to see how they may need to change to reflect agility. The main conclusions reached at the end of the workshop were, as I recall:

- Little needed change.
- Agility was more about how the various components were used (planning, risk, stakeholder management) and behaviours.
- Some changes were suggested, mostly about reflecting behaviours, e.g. in the description of leadership.

This chapter will focus on what agility looks like when *applied to* project management techniques and tools, both individually and when techniques are combined.

Most of what you will find in Chapters 5, 6 and 7 will be applicable to projects, programmes and portfolios. To avoid the cumbersome use of 'projects (programmes and portfolios)' I will stick to using the term project.

Agility means integration

In Chapter 2 when introducing a framework for project agility I was clear that it was not a magic bullet.

Examine consistently successful organizations, sports teams and individuals, the military and so on. You will find their success is built on many factors woven together. The diver Tom Daley has spoken and written of this training regime, which is way more than just going to the pool and practising dives and includes:

- gym work;
- diving movements in the gym;
- diving practice in the pool;
- diet;
- psychological coaching;
- and knitting!

He regards his diving as a mix of the technical and the behavioural and has written in his autobiography about how mental resilience is just as critical as his considerable technical competence.

How very like projects and while there is no magic bullet, you can model an approach to provide a *framework* for the many factors that play a role in project success or failure. My favourite, well tried and trusted, is People/Process/Tools. These three elements are interdependent. But looking at each in turn provides a simple structure as a starting point.

To start then, what are the components of each?

Figure 5.2: People aspects of project management

Figure 5.3: Process aspects of project management

60 Agile Beyond IT

Figure 5.4: Tools supporting project management

The elements in each of these figures (5.2–5.4) can be combined into a project management framework for agility, which will then allow you to integrate:

- the organizational aspects (how the hinterland interacts with the portfolio(s), programmes and projects), for example how governance and assurance may be adapted for agility; both internal and external interactions;
- the various behavioural aspects of delivering projects;
- portfolio management and enterprise project management office (EPMO) processes, techniques, behaviours and relationships;
- programme management processes, techniques, behaviours and relationships;
- project management processes, techniques, behaviours and relationships;
- technology that supports projects and provides a bridge with the rest of the organization;
- guidance on use of the framework, e.g. for different size/scope projects and programmes;
- mandatory components such as organizational governance requirements.

Figure 5.5 offers a suggestion for the components of the project management framework.

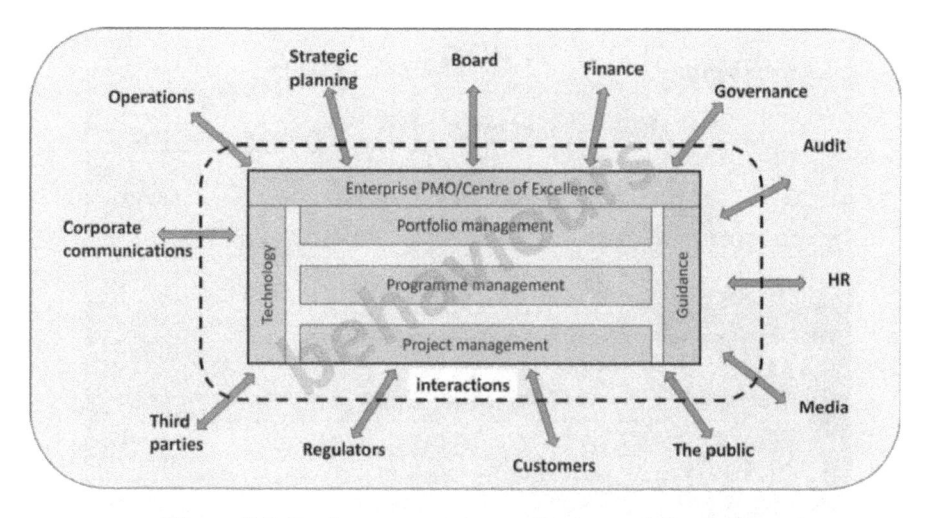

Figure 5.5: Project management framework for agility

The content of the framework should not simply reproduce standards, such as project management change control. Instead, the framework should show how each component is adapted to the organization and how they can be used within it.

N.B. Some aspects are likely to be mandatory. For example, change control and the framework will show the levels of approval and the approval route.

Culture and behaviour

Remember my organizational culture iceberg from Chapter 4?

How people throughout the organization behave impacts any organization's effectiveness. Let's look at disaster stories.

The FiReControl project story
In 2011 the UK's National Audit Office published a report into the FiReControl project.[8] The project aimed to improve the resilience, efficiency and technology of the Fire and Rescue Service by replacing 46 local control rooms with a network of nine purpose-built regional control centres, using a national computer system to handle calls, mobilize equipment and manage incidents. When cancelled, the estimated cost to date was £245 million, with a completion estimate of £635 million – more than five times the original estimate of £120 million.

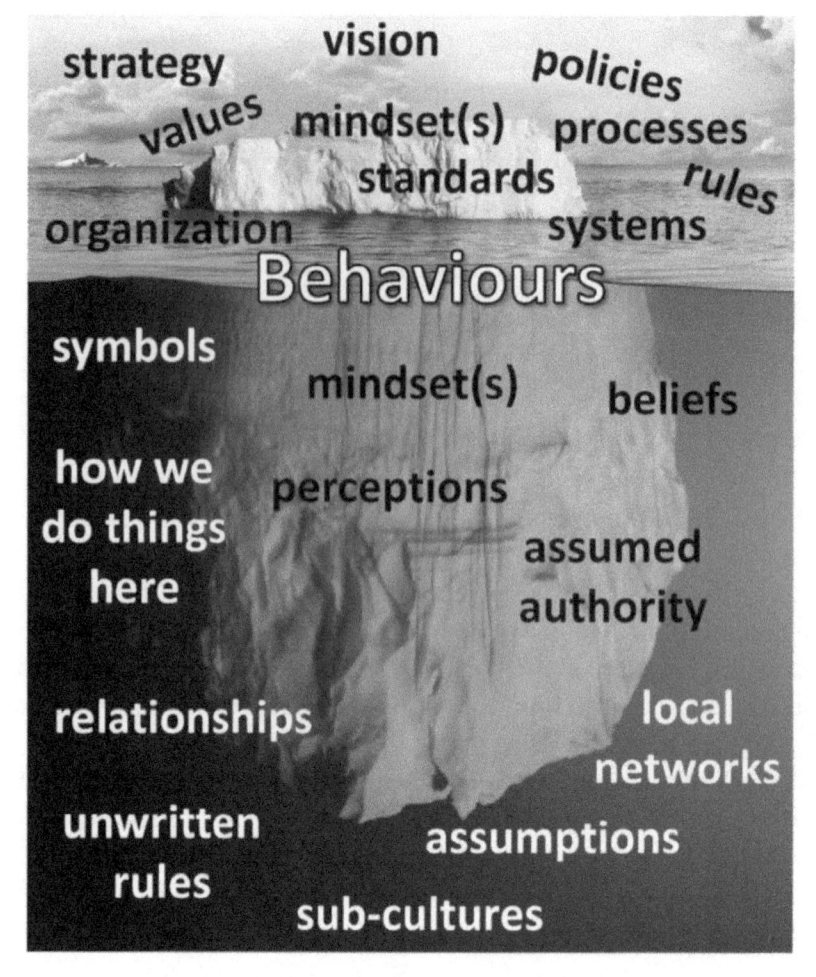

Figure 5.6: The organizational culture iceberg

Public statements, such as interviews on the BBC, indicated that mistakes had been made and that procedures would need to be reviewed and improved. Or words to that effect. The report told a different story. In a nutshell, the project:

- failed to gain the support of nor incentivize its key stakeholders;
- had no overall ownership of requirements;
- set up governance was too complex and then operated poorly;
- failed to provide leadership with multiple changing Senior Responsible Owners;

- failed to properly establish organization and responsibilities;
- had poor contract design and management.

Conclusion: there was little evidence that the standards, guidelines and procedures were at fault. Rather, the people who should have exercised control from the top down failed to follow the best practice. So the failures were behavioural, not procedural.

These tales are not limited to the project world; increasingly, examples of financial scandals and civil engineering disasters have highlighted how the culture of organizations has led to people behaving in damaging ways. Often to gain short-term commercial advantage or benefit.

Sometimes a culture can allow a company to sleepwalk into catastrophe. Kodak, a giant of the photography industry in the 20th century, filed for bankruptcy in 2012. In short, according to research by Kotter and others, the Board ignored the emerging digital technology, refusing to believe that film would be replaced, and so rapidly. Even when early innovation, which could have given them a lead, was done by their own engineers.

It is clear that organizational culture significantly influences the behaviours of people at all levels. With agility, organizational culture is at the very core of value delivery or wasted investment if mishandled.

Some years ago, I shared several conference platforms with Steve Messenger, former Chair of the Agile Business Consortium. A key message he would give was that *agile is a state of mind... the mindset*. Mindset is the set of attitudes and beliefs that affects how *you* think, feel and behave.

Agility therefore is 'of the head and the heart'. I know that to some that will sound very wishy washy but in fact it is well supported by neuroscience, and is worth a little exploration.

Projects, especially those involving change, often make people uncomfortable. They like the comfort of familiar business-as-usual, they like what they know. It is the prospect of major change which makes us uncomfortable, even fearful.

Neuroscience has shown that even the most stoical of us *always* responds to 'new' with the emotion of surprise, even if only momentarily; it is the entry point to our emotional reaction. We are hard wired for this because all responses are controlled in our brains firstly, if fleetingly, by a small area called the amygdala; one of two almond-shaped clusters of nuclei located deep in the cerebrum of the brain. The amygdala performs a primary role in the processing of memory, decision making and emotional responses (including fear, anxiety and aggression).

Initial reaction to 'new' →	Trust
	Excitement
	Surprise
	Anger
	Shame
	Sadness
	Fear

Response: toward Fear or Trust?

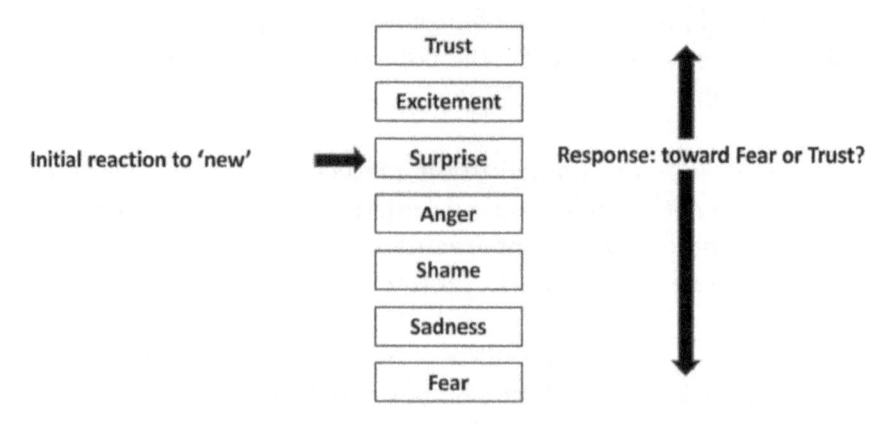

Figure 5.7: The emotional scale and the response to 'new'

At one time, those studying the human brain considered the amygdala to be a link to our distant evolutionary past. It was misnamed as our 'lizard' brain, but is considered to have an ancient function, and the amygdala's function is thought to be important to survival. If there is a threat, an animal will automatically react defensively, in some way – to flee, hide, even freeze. It is probably not surprising that the emotional scale has more responses towards fear than towards trust.

Hence, this is why people are more comfortable with the status quo – the known, than change – the unknown. And why, in order to encourage them to embrace change, you need first to remove their fear.

> **Key point:** For agility to be successful, for the projectization of work, the right new mindset must be developed, and led from the Board throughout the organization.

Changing the culture for agility

So far, the importance of organizational culture has been described, and we've outlined what it typically comprises via the iceberg model.

The challenge then is to see how that model can be used to change the organizational culture to one where projects, and agility, can *thrive*.

This is probably more familiar territory as this is *management of change*, or *business/organization transformation*. A typical change management cycle is shown in Figure 5.8.

Figure 5.8: Change management cycle

- 1. Develop change business case from Strategy and review
- 2. Share the vision
- 3. Gain commitment and mobilise
- 4. Plan the journey
- 5. Implement the change
- 6. Sustain the change

The principle is simple: the organizational culture model provides a way of analysing what the culture is and how it works. If you can do this then you can identify the components that need to be modified, added or removed. It gives you a set of outcomes around which you can build a plan.

Simple? Of course not; if it was, then why do so many organizations not go on the journey? It is because

1. organizational culture is rarely simple; rather, it is both complicated and complex;
2. there are different organizational culture models and therefore different ways to analyse the culture.

The approach that I believe best fits is that of Edgar Schein. Schein's model looks at culture from the standpoint of the observer and describes organizational culture through the perspective of three elements:

- Artefacts – organizational attributes that can be seen, felt and heard by the observer. In my iceberg they are above-the-waterline items.
- Espoused values – the professed 'culture' of an organization, e.g. company slogans, mission, vision and values. These would also normally be above the waterline.
- Basic underlying assumptions – this is anything under the surface in the iceberg model.

Another model commonly used to define organizational culture is McKinsey's 7Ss organization design model shown below.

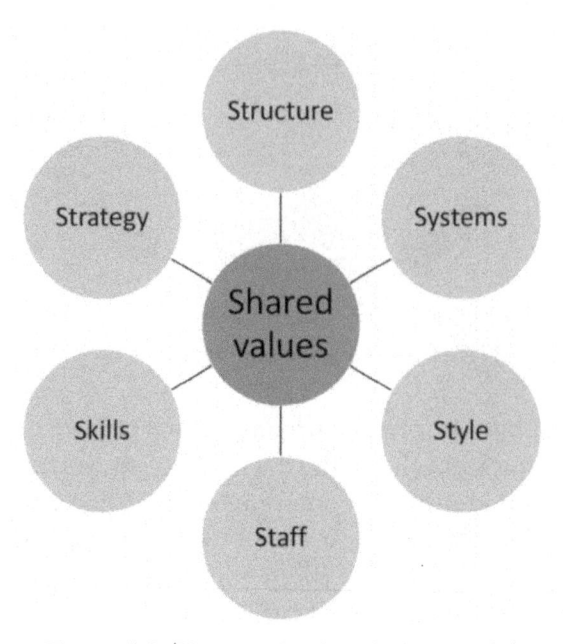

Figure 5.9: 7Ss organization design model

This can be a useful model for analysis. It has much in common with the OrgPM Framework™ components. A word of caution, however: this model was developed as an organization *design* tool. It would be easy to miss the nuances of the below-the-surface attributes of culture.

My suggestion would be to:

- use Schein's typology;
- use the McKinsey 7S model; and
- reflect the visible and invisible characteristics of the iceberg model.

In Chapter 9 I will show how this approach forms part of *becoming agile*.

Leadership and professionalism

When I started my project journey in the 1980s, the stereotypical project manager (which included me) was a control freak who wanted close control over everything and most things had to be done their way. A very autocratic style of leadership which in many project managers never varied. People in teams always had to adjust to the project manager, which suited some but alienated and de-motivated others – with a damaging impact on projects and people alike. It's the modern equivalent of galley slaves being whipped until they cheer up.

At that time, I had neither the knowledge nor language of different leadership styles or personality types. I simply knew that you had to adapt to different people and situations. At times persuading and encouraging, and at others wielding the proverbial baseball bat.

Realization also dawned that there were influential people around the project and/or impacted by it. These, who later became labelled as stakeholders, were usually more senior than me. And yet they could be managed, i.e. getting them to do or behave as I needed them to. Well, most of the time. Yes, you can manage upwards.

More on stakeholder management later in this chapter.

When it comes to bringing agility to leadership, I believe there are four main factors:

- the *mindset* that agile leaders either have or develop;
- the *environment* to support leadership agility;
- the default agile leadership *behaviour* (rather than style); and
- professionals *adapting* their leadership to the needs of the moment.

Agile leaders' mindset

There are so many views on what makes an agile leader. To my mind they confuse management, leadership, even personality types, with the characteristics of agility. For example, I have been assessed several times against the four colour personality types, which (and please bear in mind there are various versions) can be characterized simply as:

- Red: Let's do it now!
- Yellow: Let's do it together.
- Blue: Let's do it properly.
- Green: Let's do it caringly.

At different times and in different circumstances I have been assessed as both highly red and highly yellow and even as blue and green. I am not surprised that one client referred to me (I think… and hope approvingly) as a consultant chameleon.

The mindset

Mindset is to an individual what culture is to an organization. It arises from the set of beliefs, experiences and influences in our lives. I was going to say that it influences how we think and behave but it's better to say it allows us to think, react, behave as we do. Rather than driving inevitable behaviour, bereft of choice.

While mindset is individual, it is often shared within a community, e.g. the C level in an organization. But there may be a number of, if not numerous, mindsets. This is why mindset is the only component of the iceberg model that specifically occurs both above and below the waterline.

Remembering again Steve Messenger's view that agile is a state of mind, it is surprising that the Agile Manifesto makes no mention of mindset. Although many would say it is clearly implied, and the question has to be asked:

Can there be agility without an agile mindset?

But why is this question posed in this section on leadership? Firstly, because embracing agility means moving away from or at least modifying a bureaucratic organization type. Secondly, to embrace agility, leadership from the C-suite down need to *get* agility both in their head and heart.

Take a look at some of the most successful, fast-growing e-commerce and new technology companies, such as Amazon. A common factor is that as organizations they avoid the structured, rigidly hierarchical bureaucratic model. Instead they exhibit the characteristics of an *adhocracy*: a fluid, adaptive organization, operating as almost the opposite of a bureaucracy. The term was coined by Warren Bennis in his 1968 book, *The Temporary Society*, and taken up in *Future Shock* by Alvin Toffler.

Julian Birkinshaw and Jonas Ridderstråle looked at why an organization might choose between Bureaucratic, Meritocratic and Adhocracy organizations.[9] They linked adhocracy to agility, since fluidity and adaptability are key to both, and showed that organizations do not become adhocracies by accident but by design – building the mindsets and using the energy of their *leadership* to make it happen.

> **Key point:** Progress towards agility must be led and sustained from the top.

What then does a mindset for leadership agility look like? Consider the following set of questions:

- Do I ensure my teams maintain a continual focus on value?
- Do I encourage collaboration, autonomy and flexibility?
- Do I take considered risks and allow my team to as well?
- Do I expect and accept mistakes, so long as learning occurs?
- Do I see evidence of judgement improvements over time?
- Do I accept and respond rapidly to change that assures or enhances value?
- Do I understand what skills teams will need in the future?
- Do I welcome and take onboard feedback?

An apocryphal story about the late Colin Powell, former US Secretary of State. In that role he had a number of interns. He asked one to produce for him a report on a specific subject. The enthusiastic young intern duly went off and a few days later presented the report. A short while later Colin Powell sent for the intern. He observed that the report was not what he had asked for. The intern turned green and muttered 'oh shxx'. Colin Powell smiled slightly and responded, 'that's ok, you're allowed one oh shxx.'

Agility is after all about learning from mistakes, not just the freedom to make them.

The stage is now set, having seen what agile leadership is not and what the mindset underlying it is. The next thing is to describe the default leadership style.

But just before I do, a word of caution. Do not confuse leadership with engagement. Leadership is concerned with providing vision and direction for the project and getting people to go there. Engagement is about participation, which could be passive. How often have you experienced people join a meeting but contribute nothing? Leaders lead.

Hands-off leadership

The default agile leadership behaviour can be termed *hands-off leadership*. Let's have a look at what that means.

You may be a parent. If so, you may remember the experience of helping a child to ride a bike. Imagine the scene...

> That fateful moment when the stabilizers are removed. Still the parent is holding lightly onto the back of the child or part of the bike, as the child pedals slowly. Now imagine taking your hand away and the child goes wobbling a little unsteadily at first.

As the parent, what are you doing? Did you stop when you took your hand away?

Or did you run along a little behind the wobbling bike?

If the former, what happens if there is a bush, a lamp-post, a dog or another child in the way? By now you are too far away to intervene should a threat occur.

But if you are in touch you can intervene if you need to... or are asked to.

Hopefully all will be well and the wobbling reduces while the child's confidence and capability grows. You can still be in touch but you can back off a little more to give them space to grow further.

72 Agile Beyond IT

> **Key point:** The essential of agile leadership behaviours is being in touch sufficiently to intervene at need or on request. It is also closely related to how you empower a team.

How does this translate to projects? Here are two examples, one from within a project and one from outside.

Example: Supermarket change programme

Figure 5.10: Supermarket check-out

The supermarket change programme was a core part of the chain's Store Transformation portfolio. The key outcome was new point-of-sale (PoS) equipment, check-outs to you and me, in every store across their three categories: neighbourhood, high street and out-of-town. The new check-outs would be a step change in capability. While it would build on the system being replaced, the step change was enabling the capture of Big Data to support marketing and stock control. Plus being able to take advantage of much faster data links, provision of which was another part of the Store Transformation portfolio.

Each check-out comprised the hardware with accompanying PoS software. Both were state of the art, from well-regarded specialist suppliers. The programme's projects were:

- Business case and high-level requirements prioritization. This was authorized pre-programme formation.
- Procurement (hardware and software).
- PoS software development.
- Hardware (check-out) configuration, including integration of delivered PoS software.
- Pilots in three regions and all three store types.
- Phase 1 roll-out.
- Phase 2 roll-out, including upgrades.
- Phase 3 roll-out, including upgrades.

The Retail Operations director would be the sponsor and formed a Programme Board from members of the Retail Operations Board, IT, Finance and the Enterprise Portfolio Office.

The main Board approved an agile approach to the programme for the following reasons:

- Requirements were quite mature (from the old system and much work by the Marketing and Logistics departments, which formed part of the Programme Board and team).
- The hardware solution mostly only required configuration to the digital connections, interfaces with core systems, e.g. for price changes or remote software upgrades, and for branding.
- The software solution, while requiring significant configuration (branding, workflows, marketing, price change processes, triggers and rules), was expected to mostly use built-in functionality. Estimated additional 10% functionality.
- The installation approach was well tried and trusted, although not at the scale proposed.
- The chosen PoS software supplier had a highly mature agile software development capability and would provide training and coaching.
- An agile coach was to support at the programme level.

- The company's project, programme and portfolio management capability maturity was assessed at Level 4. This included an Enterprise PMO, which also led the project centre of excellence and the project delivery community.

The main Board approved a business case which fixed the time and cost and specified a minimum scope (for the software this was at the Epic level), based on prioritized requirements.

Within the Board approval it authorized the sponsor personally with the budget, time and scope targets/constraints plus a contingency. The programme board was instructed to anticipate and clear obstacles.

Contracts and associated purchase orders identified programme and project-specific cost codes. Finance and the EPMO tracked incoming invoices to ensure they would be accrued correctly. Project managers were required to only validate each invoice. Finance and the EPMO provided tracking and reporting.

The EPMO, Finance and programme manager negotiated a level of governance more reliant on management by exception. Software tools enabled both dashboards and deep dives to be undertaken.

In short, an environment was established in which agility could thrive. Agile leadership in this programme in essence was the delegation of authority to the sponsor, programme and project managers and development teams. Each was empowered to make decisions within clear scope and flex ways of working within the minimal assurance framework, agreed with the EPMO. Technology enabled progress data to be captured by the EPMO, who then analysed and presented dashboards, trend analysis and, when requested, deep dives.

The main impact of the delegation and assurance framework was as follows:

- To free the sponsor to clear roadblocks and stakeholder manage at the executive level.

- To enable the programme manager to ensure integration across the programme's projects, maintaining the integrity of the emerging capability while maintaining an overview, both snapshot and trends in programme and project progress.
- To enable each project manager to liaise with line managers, e.g. regarding subject matter experts (SMEs). They ensured that project data was accurate and up to date, 'walked the job' and managed earned value.
- Development teams were empowered to make decisions within their delivery scope and time targets, e.g. on detailed requirements, design and product configuration or development.

Behaviourally, the biggest challenge early on was to get the SMEs used to taking decisions, such as exactly how a card payment function would work. They were confident in their choices, but were used to referring to their line managers for decisions. In parallel, relevant line managers were initially uncomfortable but were included in 'demos'. Later, most stopped attending regularly as they became more confident in the outputs from their people seconded to the programme.

It might be thought that agility would be most obvious in the PoS software project. Yes, it used Scrum, in fact for a period, three Scrum teams. Jira was used for developing Epics and user stories, prioritizing them and allocating to Sprints. Also there were agile development experts used to working collaboratively and coaching their client's people.

And yet, albeit hands-off, the PoS software project received the most programme manager and sponsor attention as it had the highest level of uncertainty and expected development effort.

The check-out configuration challenges were mostly technical and well understood, relating to store-related constraints such as use of space, power, digital connections, ergonomics for staff usage and customer behaviour. This project team were provided with clarity of outcomes, schedule and, in effect, were allowed to get on with it. Again in hands-off style.

The team planning the roll-outs were well experienced and given help to work at scale. They again were given the freedom to plan the most cost and time-effective roll-outs.

From an example of leadership agility throughout a programme, including from the Board level, the next example focuses on events in a single project. Here also the organizational culture plays a key role in the project manager's leadership and decision-making agility.

Example: Leadership and assumed authority
This is an example taken from an airport. A perfect case of operations trump projects every time, given that the airport operates for passengers for around 18 hours each day. Many projects can of course progress without impacting operations or disturbing passengers. However, some need to occur in the dead hours of the night. Talk about fixed time for a project.

There is another factor involved relevant to this example. Tucked up in bed are the director of terminal operations and their senior management. Tonight an engineering project manager is overseeing contractors replacing parts of the air-conditioning system on a three-month out-of-hours project now two weeks from completion; several issues have used up the available float. A major project is dependent on this one completing on time.

During tonight's installation, the contractors discovered early on that several connections for the control system are corroded and a control unit also needs to be replaced. The contractors say they have spare connections but a control box is back at their depot, about a 30 minutes' drive away. The cost of the additional kit amounts to £3000. The project manager has no formal authority for additional spend. However, having assessed that the new control unit can be sent for on time while the remaining installation takes place, they authorize the additional work and complete a change log accordingly. The contractor, who has a four-year relationship with the airport, accepts the informal authority.

The installation completes on time and the project manager submits the change for formal approval by the senior engineering and terminal operations managers, who both confirm the change.

Two days later, there is the weekly terminal projects review meeting, which operates mostly by exception. The project manager is expected to and does present a justification for their assumption of authority. They described their rapid assessment of the time, cost and risk to meet the objective. The risk being two-fold: the risk of not approving the change and still not completing the work. There were paragraphs stopping installation and impacting the start of the major dependent project (a project they had no direct responsibility for… and yet…). Their report was accepted and they were congratulated.

The background here is that because many projects are done out of normal working hours delegated authority could not in practice predict the multiplicity of challenges that may be faced. The project professionals are expected to use their judgement, even assuming a level of authority they do not have. Remembering the Colin Powell story, he would no doubt have been proud.

The culture was for project professionals to take reasonable risks and be supported in doing so. Of course, there is a potential downside if they get it wrong too often (Colin Powell again). These project professionals were selected for their ability to work in this way and were fully briefed on that expectation. Not all project managers would be happy with such a culture. Neither would many organizations with what Julian Birkenshaw would refer to as the *bureaucratic mindset.*

👍 Agile leaders know when to assume authority, even when they don't have it.

Virtual leadership

I had always planned to discuss virtual leadership in this book. Given the gigantic impact on work occasioned by the Covid-19 pandemic, it has become and remains a key working approach.

The drivers and enablers for virtual working and virtual leadership have been growing. A 2017 and therefore pre-Covid-19 report, commissioned by the workspace provider Regus,[10] provides some intriguing evidence:

- 50% of workers report they work outside of the main office at least 2.5 days per week, of which 36% say this is at home.
- 27% of workers say their commute is a waste of time.
- A US report shows that one in three workers choose to become freelance to gain flexibility.
- Canadian research shows that 79% of freelancers are happier with their work–life balance.
- 91% of the 18–44 age group in the UK had smartphones, much higher than China (62%) or the EU average (61%).

The Regus report concludes that the (then) much more modest amount of homeworking as the percentage of the total shows that 'home working is seriously damaging for productivity and doesn't convey a professional image, with family members, with pets and household noises, disturbing calls and concentration levels… workers report that at home they are unable to access key office equipment and a reliable and speedy internet connection.'

Such an emphasis at the time by a workspace provider may be a case of 'well, they would say that wouldn't they'. With apologies to Mandy Rice-Davies. Then along came the tragedy of Covid-19 and everything changed.

Drivers	Enablers
Cost saving	Broadband speed and availability
Pressure to change the work–life balance	VoIP
Greater proportion of freelancers	Mobile network speeds
Demand for increased working flexibility	Smartphone apps
Need to retain good people	Collaborative tools
Movement towards agility	More cost-effective webcams
Movement towards collaborative working	Improved security of cloud-based data

Figure 5.11: Drivers and enablers for virtual working

Working mostly freelance for 15 years and as a consultant for over 10 years, I am very used to remote working. Mostly from home but also in business centres, hotel rooms and, perhaps at last resort, coffee shops. That kind of agility, for that is what it is, is clearly commonplace. Even planning ahead for a business trip needs to not just include transport and accommodation but also the ability to work, take and make calls and join virtual meetings.

Even working from home must be planned, and the home environment – what others in a virtual meeting will see of your home – is a factor in how you present yourself. What people wear, their home's décor, kids and pets have become comedy staples to help us face Covid-19.

> Several years ago, I was advising a video technologies company on developing collaborative relationships with clients. There were sound commercial imperatives for this. This included a few trips to Atlanta, called the city in the trees, but also many video calls. One very warm summer's day I was working in the shade in the garden. With a strong wifi signal, I decided to remain there for the virtual meeting. While there was some surprise at my moving green backdrop, when I pointed out I could see the same out of the windows behind them and wanted the same ambience, everybody laughed… fortunately.

👍 Assess and know your audience.

This story highlights one of the many challenges of virtual working and virtual leadership. The excellent *Virtual Leadership* by Dr Penny Pullan[11] suggests the following challenges:

- Trust takes longer to build – and can disappear rapidly.
- Multiple projects can distract people.
- Virtual meetings are tedious.
- Conflict is less visible.
- Fewer 'water cooler' moments.
- The need for shorter sessions.
- It is not a level playing field.
- It's easy to be invisible.

To which I would add:

- Performance management of remote workers.
- Resistance to virtual technology among some workers, becoming less as more people get used to it/need it.

It has to be said that some of the challenges of virtual meetings, and therefore virtual leadership, are the same as face to face:

- Over-long meetings.
- Lack of agenda.
- People not listening.
- Poor meeting leadership.

What the pandemic seems to have done is highlight the need to balance virtual with face-to-face working.

> During a coffee break while on a speaker panel for Nottingham University Business School in 2020, one speaker, a director of a UK car company, observed that many people were clamouring for at least some time in the office as they 'missed their colleagues'. Even while others, especially those more at risk, were expressing concerns about returning to the office. This in itself is a leadership challenge.

How then does agility apply to virtual leadership? Best to start with the questions that test leadership agility:

- Do I ensure my teams maintain a continual focus on value?
    - Were the meeting purpose and outcomes clear before and during the meeting?
        - How was this done?
    - Was there a brief review at the end?
        - For example, using a virtual poll which also provides data for learning.
        - Were people asked how they felt about the meeting?

- Were the right people taking part? If not, why not and what can you do next time?
- Did everybody need to be there throughout the meeting?
- Could it have been compartmentalized to allow for focused engagement?
- How long was the meeting planned for? Was it right?
- Do I encourage collaboration, autonomy and flexibility?
  - Probably the hardest tightrope to tread.
  - Were people engaged? How? For example, encouragement, allowing them time, use of polls. How did you assess their engagement?
  - How did people make suggestions and ask questions?
    - spoken;
    - on a virtual board;
    - open polls;
    - text in a chat session.
- Do I take considered risks and allow them too?
  - What did you do to allow/encourage off-the-wall ideas?
  - How did people express these? Spoken, contributed to a virtual board? Chat session text question?
- Do I expect and accept mistakes if they are learned from?
  - How were ideas and suggestions expressed?
  - How was criticism handled?
- Do I accept and respond rapidly to change that ensures or enhances value?
  - Another tricky area as meeting purpose/scope is often questioned.
  - How was this managed? Was it disruptive? Was it valid?
  - How did the challenger(s) react? What impact has that on them and the team?
- Do I understand what skills teams will need in the future?
  - Do they understand how best to use videoconferencing?
- Do I welcome and take on board feedback?
  - Was feedback sought?
    - Before, e.g. about the purpose/scope/outcomes.
    - During, e.g. meeting review.
    - After.
    - How much feedback? If little or none, is that a concern or a good thing?

○ How was unsolicited feedback reacted to?

All these questions (and their answers) offer a mixture of useful prompts for meeting planning (virtual or otherwise) and learning about the behaviours established in your project's culture.

> **Key point:** Agility means discipline as well as flexibility.

Agility in project teams

Julius Caesar knew a thing or two about team agility. Yes, he was known for moving legions rapidly to out-manoeuvre enemy forces. But Roman legions were self-organized to a significant extent. Remember, the only communications were by the despatch riders of the day. A message and the response could take days and often weeks; therefore, the vision and operating boundaries and the general strategy had to be made crystal clear. Julius had to trust his troops, from legates down to legionaries, to perform as trained. They were:

- clearly briefed and functioned as units of varying sizes from cohort to century to legion;
- self-organized even in cohorts and could operate with a degree of independence on patrol, and roles flexed e.g. following injury;
- highly trustful due to reliance on their cohort, century and legion;
- collaborative;
- continuously trained and retrained.

My 2020 LinkedIn article 'Julius Caesar's Agile Conquest of Gaul 58 to 52BC' goes into more detail. What struck me most was the degree of self-organization.

However, top answer or not, and having scrutinized many books, blogs and articles, plus my own interpretation, here are my characteristics of an agile project team:

- has clear purpose;
- is self-organizing/autonomous;
- is empowered but knows its boundaries;
- will make decisions;
- has effective communication;

- engenders trust;
- operates continuous improvement;
- exhibits mostly collaborative behaviours;
- is adaptable including role flexibility within the project structure;
- emphasizes team over individual.

I almost added *is cross-functional*, but that is commonly true of a project team in general rather than a characteristic of agility.

A challenge I had when compiling my list of characteristics is that most such lists are in the software development context, even when they were labelled project management. *We* is commonly heard in teams that exhibit agility. Listen for it as an indicator that the individuals co-identify as team members, a pre-requisite for agility. An absence of *we* should set alarm bells ringing. There is a good deal of selflessness in members of mature agile teams.

The challenges of building team agility

Let me indulge not in fantasy football but fantasy agile team selection:

- My high-performing team would exhibit all the characteristics of an agile team.
- The subject matter experts would never have to ask for clarification or a decision outside of the team.
- The technical specialists would be the best.
- The delivery people would be superbly experienced.
- I would have all team members for as long as they were promised to me.
- The team would be passionate about the project and its vision, and well versed in working practices.

And then I wake up. The real world is never a perfect place. Project managers seldom get the perfect resources. Turn the points above upside down and you have the most common challenges.

In the real world, and I could have included this under *Hands-off leadership*, there are dynamics at play in all teams, in all organizations. Being in a team and/or leading one means you need to have awareness of these dynamics because they, like organizational culture, impact how people behave, or change their behaviour.

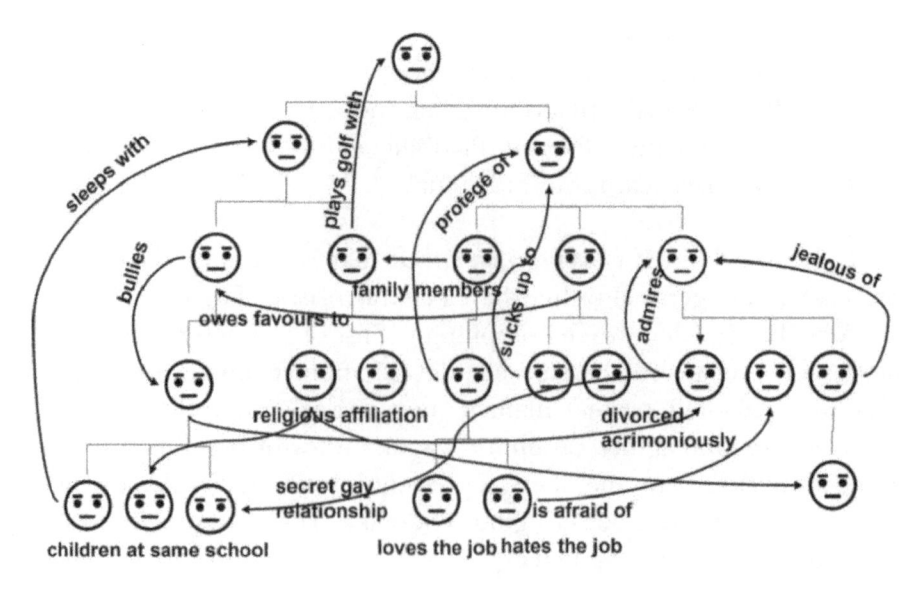

Figure 5.12: Real-life relationships

A jaundiced view perhaps. But team dynamics, to continue the iceberg culture model, are the undercurrents at work. They reflect how individuals are feeling about and interacting personally with each other.

Preparing to build an agile team

A criticism often made of agile is that of course it can succeed well *if*, and it's a *big if*, you have the perfect team in a supportive project landscape. Which is unfair, as the old joke has it:

> *Woman to man in New York*: Can you tell me how to get to Carnegie Hall?
>
> *Man in New York*: Lady, you gotta practise!

But agility is about adaptation so, like a good scout, project managers should be prepared. Especially for frankly predictable risks at the beginning of a project.

To build an effective agile team you need to plan to manage both inside the project and in its landscape. Let us take a look at that journey.

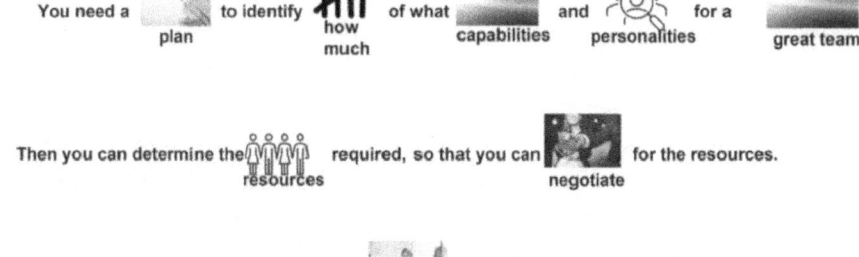

You need a [plan] to identify [how much] of what [capabilities] and [personalities] for a great team.

Then you can determine the [resources] required, so that you can [negotiate] for the resources.

Just in case you need to find out who can provide [back up]

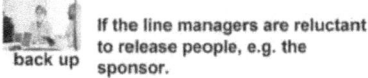

If the line managers are reluctant to release people, e.g. the sponsor.

You could also see what the project might [do for] them for mutual benefit.

Figure 5.13: Finding the agile team

Growing and sustaining the team

We are back to Kotter again and the need to keep the energy going. The key is to keep going what should by now be in place:

- C-suite leadership actively supporting agility.
- An active sponsor, suitably empowered.
- 'Hands-off' leadership at portfolio, programme and project levels.
- The team operating agile behaviours to maintain the characteristics of agility.

It's not just about getting to Carnegie Hall – once, but again and again and again. Which means the following team success factors:

- Visibly delivering value.
- Being open both inside and outside the team, even when things go wrong.
- Being the team, maintaining internal and external relationships, e.g. keeping the *we* going.
- Regularly reviewing not just what you are doing but how well you are doing it.
- Building learning back in.

Team performance management

It is often written that in self-organizing teams, leadership is shared: an ambiguous statement taken too literally by some. In the project space this simply does not work. Without re-playing the *Leadership* sections above, it is possible, even desirable, for any member of a project team to *at times* manage downwards, upwards and outwards. This does not create delusions of grandeur, meaning everybody in the team is *the* leader.

For agility, everybody in the team is looking out for everyone else, supporting them. Sometimes that support means spotting less than optimal performance, pointing it out and helping the struggling team member.

However, the one person in a team who is *accountable* for managing performance is the team's leader. It is their job. Whether that be programme, project or work package manager, Scrum Master or whatever. The agile team leader will be looking to the team success factors and monitoring those, which might include:

- progress of outputs and outcomes against plan including trend;
- quality of outputs and outcomes against acceptance criteria;
- costs against plan;
- stakeholder reactions;
- working approach effectiveness including trend;
- team morale;
- individual morale.

It is also their role more than any other person in the team to spot and manage sub-optimal performance and they are accountable for doing so outside their team, e.g. project manager to programme manager, programme manager to sponsor.

How they manage is a matter for the manager's toolbox and the ability to adapt to the needs of the project, the team, the person and the moment. Personally, I would prefer to coach than wield a baseball bat. But there is one software company senior account manager I shall not mention, in front of whom I placed a baseball bat – purely as a symbol of what would happen to the contract if his company did not stop playing win–lose with my client. After all, he who pays the piper…

The self model

Earlier in this section I made reference to my *self model*, which needs some explanation. Around 2008, I started to think a lot about team-building techniques. These usually focused on the group, how to bring them together and meld them into a team – such as through forming, storming, norming and performing. But I wondered whether there was a viewpoint from the individual. In looking at teams I realized that an individual progressively gives more of them *selves* to a team the longer they are in it and the more value they place on that team. I doubt I am the only one to have noticed this but I could not find a model that suited.

The self model is my attempt to show how an individual may progressively *sublimate* themselves to a team.

> *Incidentally, Sigmund Freud considered sublimation a sign of maturity that allows people to behave in civilized and acceptable ways. This process can lead people to pursue activities that are better for their health or engage in behaviours that are positive, productive, and creative. This is particularly suited to working as part of a team.*

What arose from observations, reading and conversations is the following model. At present it is only supported by anecdotal evidence but could suit some post-graduate research.

Behaviour	Characteristics
Self-centred	- Role in the team is defined. - Not yet confident in the role. - Focuses on own needs while learning team ways of working. - Limited personal interaction with other team members. - Lack of openness.
Self-reliant	- Growing confidence in own role. - Starting to form relationships with team members. - Growing openness.

| Self-sacrifice | • Fully confident in role and in place in team.
• Confident in the ways of working.
• Starting to suggest ways to improve team ways of working.
• Open and good working relationships with rest of the team.
• Working outside of own role to support other team members. |
|---|---|
| Self-sublimation | • Acts in support of the team vision and ways of working.
• Filling in for other team members.
• Reacts positively to smooth conflicts in team.
• Supports colleagues' ideas over their own. |
| Self-submergence | • Actively engages in the team vision and ways of working.
• Pro-active in supporting both individuals and the team.
• Promotes colleagues' ideas over their own. |

Figure 5.14: The self model

The model proposes the stages a person goes through as they sublimate themselves as a member of a team. My thought is that organizations could use this approach to help accelerate the effectiveness of team formation. Or to more rapidly bring a new person into an established team. Or help an individual integrate into an established team. Here is a short story.

> I had been running a transformation programme in retail finance for about a year when my best planner left and I needed to replace them. This was a challenge as the programme management office was a close-knit team of great people. During the interview for a new planner, one question I asked candidates was how would they ease themself into this established team? One candidate smiled and immediately said in his Yorkshire accent, oh I would start a curry club. The job was theirs.

Roles and responsibilities

Earlier I made reference to a review of competencies carried out several years ago by the Association for Project Management. It concluded that applying agility did not significantly change the competencies or their descriptions. It is a similar story with project management roles and responsibilities. But agility does have some impact.

- Project managers are still project managers.
- Programme managers are still programme managers.
- Workstream managers are still workstream managers.
- Sponsors (Senior Responsible Owners, Champions, call them what you will) are still sponsors.

What *is* different is how those roles are carried out, which is mostly behavioural. The role profile, which describes the type of person needed, may well change.

Under collaborative working, which is critical to agility, the nature of interactions not just within the project, but also with collaborating groups outside, should be win-win, helpful, can-do.

Agility has perhaps a greater impact on business-as-usual management roles and responsibilities in two ways. Firstly, an organization adapting to agility will require managers to be able to act more on their own initiative (as they will be more empowered) and will expect more collaborative working. Secondly, the projectization of work – the project economy – increasingly means that any (operational) manager/supervisor might be called on to lead part/all of a project. Project management will increasingly become a core management skill for any manager.

A word of caution: project management is a skill which can be learned, but levels of capability vary greatly. Which is why I keep practising my drumming skills and, while I love it, I will never be much good.

Agility and creativity

A good indicator of a culture of agility is that people are given the freedom to:

- try stuff;
- take some risks;

- be allowed to fail, in order to learn and create better outcomes;
- act beyond their pay grade with good judgement;
- put their hand up;
- disagree with someone.

> I was working in the USA with a video technology company and a major client, working with some truly talented people. They were exploring new ways of working together to make their customer-supplier projects more successful. It may sound like a cliché but good old southern hospitality was definitely the dominant culture. There had been several meetings and we did not seem to be getting anywhere. I called for a workshop to provide the time to iron out the issues and agree a new working approach.
>
> But everybody was just too nice to each other. An hour after lunch on the first day I could take it no longer and shouted out:
>
> > *Will you all stop being so nice to each other and say what you really think?!*
>
> They all stared at me in shock. After what seemed minutes but was only seconds my senior VP (vice president) client smiled and said:
>
> > *I thought you Brits were tight-arsed and stiff upper lipped, but hey you are more American than us.*
>
> It broke the ice and after a short coffee break we moved on to define a collaborative approach, both commercial and project, quite new to both organizations.

Creativity is more likely under a culture of agility so again it comes back to leadership both inside and outside projects. From which can arise:

- innovative ideas;
- encouragement of problem solving;
- better team morale and working together;
- improved productivity.

All of which lead ultimately to the creation of value.

> **Key point:** Give people the room and the freedom to speak, and creativity will follow.

Stakeholder management and communications

I have written, blogged, lectured and coached more on stakeholder management than any other project management technique. In 1992, I wrote BT's (British Telecom as then was) first guidance on managing stakeholders and communication planning.

I think it would be useful to be clear who we are talking about. APM's definition of a stakeholder is useful here: *Individuals or groups who have an interest or role in a project, programme or portfolio, or are impacted by it.*

As with agility in projects, stakeholder management is so very often badly used. A common mistake is to rush into doing some communication, perhaps to fill the silence at the very beginning of a project or to show willingness when reacting to an incident during delivery. Given that agility calls for delivery early and often, isn't this a good thing? No, as frequently this leads to the *wrong message* being given to the *wrong audience*(s) at the *wrong time* and in the *wrong way*. The result is then annoyance, alienation, opposition, derision. In short, damage to the project.

And yet a simple framework exists which I have used for almost 40 years. Its adaptability has stood the test of time and been validated. I do not claim ownership, merely its use.

Stakeholder management and communications planning framework

A simple structured approach to stakeholder management starts with five simple questions:

Why, Who, What, When and *How.*
1. *Why* do you want to communicate?
2. *Who* do you want to communicate with?
3. *What* are the messages you need to communicate?
4. *When* do you need to communicate?
5. *How* will you communicate?

The *why* are your communication objectives: what you want to achieve with your various stakeholders, e.g. steering a business through to approval, negotiating for resources, overcoming opposition to project outcomes and so on. In good agile fashion this is the value you need to focus on throughout the project.

The *who* are the stakeholders.

The *what* are the messages you need to give to them. Perhaps different ones at different times to various stakeholders, often depending on their interests.

The *when* is the timing of communications, most often driven by the schedule, e.g. you may plan to trumpet the successful delivery of a phase of the project to maintain impetus and support.

The *how* is the way or ways in which you will communicate. Do *not* do this first for the reasons I mentioned in the second paragraph of this section.

Now we can look at the stakeholder management framework, which looks like Figure 5.15.

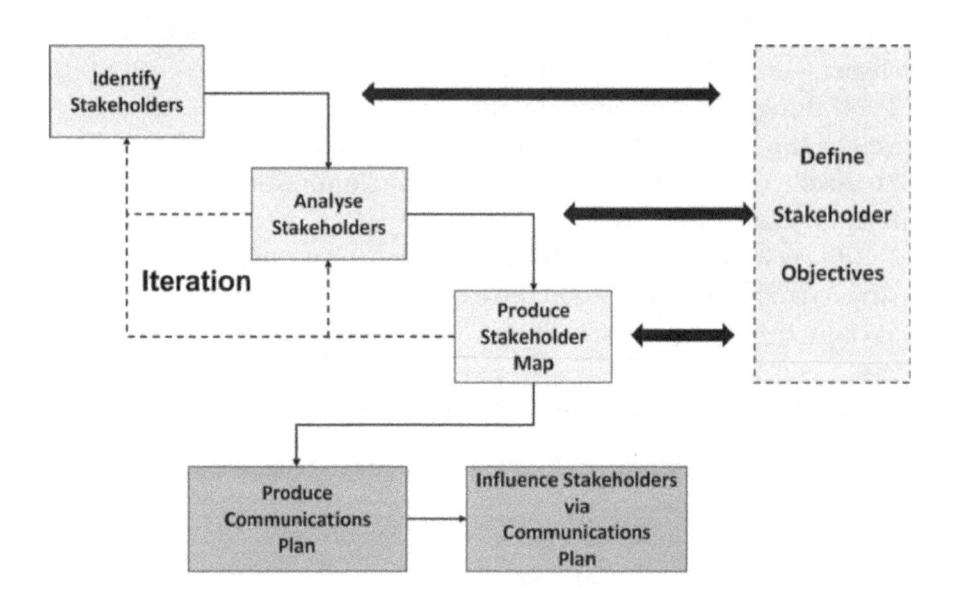

Figure 5.15: Stakeholder management framework

Identify stakeholders tells you who they are and who they are not. I have found for example that especially in the public sector, lots of folk crawl out of the woodwork pretending to have an interest in your project, or seeking one. Usually for personal political (small p) reasons. I call these *wannabees*. Identify them and then ignore them as they will waste lots of your valuable time.

This part will *not* tell you who you should focus your attention on, which comes next.

Analyse stakeholders is perhaps the engine room. This is where you learn about them by talking to them, or asking people who know them, but examining their relationship with the project. Apart from this biographical information, the simplest analysis is to determine whether they are an *Ally, Neutral* or *Opposed* to your project. Your objective should be to at least neutralize opposers, turn neutrals into allies and to have the active not passive support of allies.

The manipulative nature of this technique is emerging. From here you can enrich your analysis at need:

- What level of influence/power does each have?
- What level of energy does each have?
  - powerful and energetic allies are great;
  - powerful and energetic opposers are a significant threat (risk management again).

- Are they only interested in aspects of your project?
  - For example, the CFO is probably only interested in finance; see the story just below.
- You can increase understanding of their attitude. Opposers could be in denial, angry, frustrated, feeling ignored, be open to persuasion or negotiation.
- Then there are some key types, whom I call Sultans and Grand Viziers.
  - Sultans usually control funding;
  - Grand Viziers are the people they listen to.

And there are other nuanced analytical types.
Two words of warning, *seduction* and *security*.

- Seduction: stakeholder analysis is seductive; do not do more than you need.
- Security: you are finding out about people. Be careful how you record and store what you find out.

On that second point: agility means openness, but some information, even opinions, about opposers could be… misinterpreted. Public sector projects may be subject to the Freedom of Information Act so avoid embarrassment. Flexibility and pragmatism are also agility.

Influence

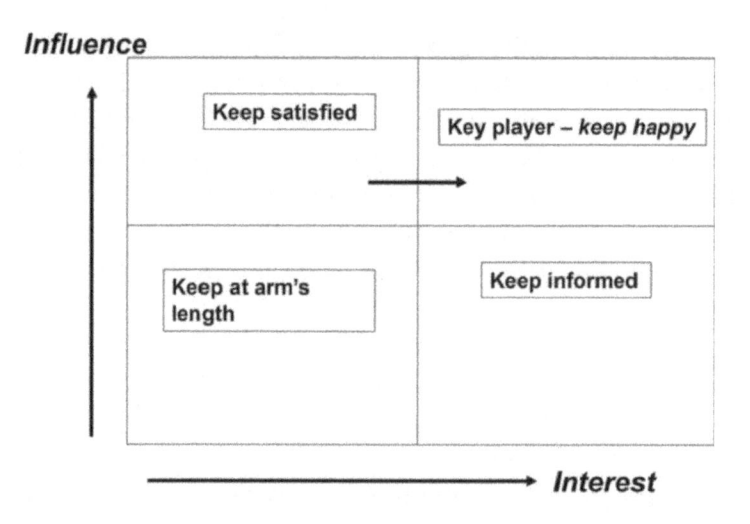

Keep satisfied	Key player – *keep happy*
Keep at arm's length	Keep informed

Interest

Figure 5.16: Stakeholder influence and interest

There are various graphical ways to plot the information, enabling you to prioritize and focus stakeholder activity. Remember that this is dynamic; levels of interest and influence may change and need to be monitored. I remember an operational manager who was very interested in a project I was leading but had no direct involvement. Initially I limited my engagement with them, until they decided to use the project as the basis of part of an MBA. Therefore, their relationship changed and they were accorded more attention.

Example: Free oil please
A professional colleague of mine started working life as a project engineer on North Sea oil rigs in the 1980s. A major growth period. At the opening of one new rig, a number of executives visited the platform and my friend was deputed to show one of them around. For over an hour he waxed lyrical on various bits of kit and boyishly enthused over their efficiency…. and cost. This cost $2m, that cost $4.5m and so on. At last, he noticed the increasingly pained expression of his VIP visitor.

Summoning courage he asked what was the matter. To which the Chief Financial Officer, for it was he (alas mostly he in those days), said: *son, I want oil out of the ground for nothing, and here you are proudly telling me how much I am losing before I can make even a dollar.*

> **Key point:** Know your audience!

Having completed your stakeholder analysis you can compile it into a *stakeholder map,* comprising the Why, Who and What.

Now you can build your communications plan, the cycle for which looks like this:

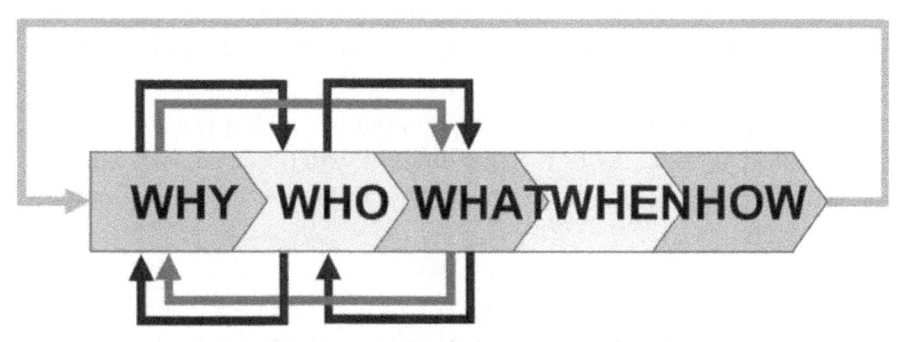

Figure 5.17: Communications planning cycle

At first sight this appears linear but notice the arrows. They allow you to iterate your analysis at need, and during the project not just at the beginning. If you have done your stakeholder identification and analysis then you have the Why, Who and the What. Now you can work out when you need to communicate and the best ways to do so.

I suggested earlier that your project schedule will greatly inform when you need to communicate, e.g.:

- pre-project in enlisting help to build the business case;
- smoothing the passage of business case approval;
- energizing the team and stakeholders at project mobilization and throughout the project;
- gaining engagement for a stage gate review;
- communicating success at major delivery milestones;
- not forgetting that reporting is also communication and a useful way to show progress to relevant stakeholders.

96 Agile Beyond IT

Finally, we come to *how* you will communicate. The channels available today are far greater than when I led my first very large communication project in the early 1990s. It was a long time ago but still provides some good learnings.

Example: BT PhONEday
On 1 August 1995 a single digit was added to UK phone numbers to provide millions of new numbers. This four-year programme, which cost BT about £80m, was called PhONEday. The communications challenge both internally and especially externally was tremendous. Here is a summary of the external plan.

The stakeholder management framework was used. The communications plan was mostly designed to build awareness in the various media and to prepare the public, businesses and public sector, e.g. alarms companies with phone-based monitoring, businesses with automated switchboards, GPs with out-of-hours emergency locums. Lots of re-configuration had to be done.

BT PhONEday external communications plan

Customers:
- Newspaper advertising
- TV and radio advertising
- Bill leaflets
- Poster campaigns
- Consumer programme features

Public services:
- NHS journal advertising
- NHS journal editorials
- NHS briefing packs
- Health professional body communications
- Contact with every GP surgery

Industries:
- Industry journal advertising
- Industry journal editorials
- Industry briefing packs
- Professional body communications
- Communication to major companies and SMEs

£11 million

Figure 5.18: BT PhONEday communications plan key components

The costs, mostly advertising on radio, TV and printed media, came to around £11m.

A few years ago, a social media marketing colleague with an interest in project management reworked my case study using social media as follows.

BT PhONEday external communications plan with social media

Customers:
- Viral marketing campaigns, Twitter, Facebook etc.
- Blogs, pop-ups
- Customer emails and SMS
- Consumer programme features
- Less TV, radio and newspaper advertising
- Poster campaigns and bill leaflets

Public services:
- NHS journal advertising and editorials
- NHS internal social media content
- NHS digital briefing packs
- Health professional body communications
- Contact with every GP surgery

£4 to 5 million

Industries:
- Industry journal advertising and journals
- Industry internal social media content
- Industry digital briefing packs
- Professional body communications and websites
- Communication to major companies and SMEs

Figure 5.19: BT PhONEday social media impact on costs

His estimate was that use of social media channels would cut the costs by at least 50%. Agility with a cost benefit.

Example: FIRe control programme – getting it wrong
One of the key conclusions of the National Audit Office report was that the programme's leadership failed to bring the key stakeholders along with them. They assumed the various regions would just buy into the vision. They did not.

Example: NHS NPfIT email project – getting it right
This much-maligned super programme actually had some great successes. Even some not looked for but very welcome outcomes. One project was the development of a new email and messaging system. One welcome benefit was mentioned to

me by a senior GP. He related that as the system could be set to send text messages to an individual patient, he found he could 'programme' it for a message saying something like... take the blue pill now. The GP used it for some patients more.... advanced in years and perhaps a little forgetful, but who were well able to use mobile phones. This GP found that hospital admissions from incorrect medication fell rapidly among older patients as a result. Truly agility at work.

On the face of it, it was a beneficial new system. And yet, part of the project was to form in effect a sales team, which toured the country to persuade individual hospitals, even GP surgeries, to use the new system – the reason being the degree of local autonomy in the NHS. That GP was a key advocate who greatly assisted communications.

Speaking of the NHS and to give a little more background, here is an intriguing example of selective communication. If members of the public were surveyed and asked if they approved of the postcode lottery of NHS provision, the result would be – has been – resounding opposition. If members of the public were surveyed and asked whether they approved of provision based on local need, the answer would be – has been – resounding approval.

Local provision and the postcode lottery are just two ways of describing the same thing. Communication is a powerful tool, for good or ill.

I have unsurprisingly left out a great deal of detail and options. The key to being agile is to determine what communication approach is best and adapt to the needs of the project during its life-cycle.

Assessing communications success

Communications planning is just that, and there needs to be a way of checking it is working. The results of communication are commonly behavioural, e.g. persuading a senior manager not to put roadblocks in the way of your project. Therefore, they are usually not as easily trackable and measureable as a shop ready for opening or a software upgrade released into live operation. However, another advantage of the semi-structured approach described is that the stakeholder objectives and associated key messages provide the means of defining success criteria:

- Objective: winning senior management support for the project business case.
  - Have you obtained either individual sign-off or tangible evidence of support, for example an email to a business case decision maker?
- Objective: gain and maintain customer user satisfaction with programme progress.
  - Have you regularly surveyed the users and what is the response?
  - Is there regular customer account management and is feedback sought?

Example: UK telco professional services
Customer satisfaction was a key customer relationship management objective for both account directors in sales and the professional services team. This was important as happy customers are more likely to return for more business and recommend you. Secondly, when issues do arise, a happy customer is more likely to make some allowances, so long as remedial action is taken. There were three main components to gauge customer satisfaction:

- Customer feedback to the sales team.
- Customer feedback to the project managers.
- Customer team feedback between customer/professional service project team members.

Project highlight reports had two means of reflecting customer satisfaction. Firstly, one of the RAG (Red, Amber, Green) status flags represented customer satisfaction and was based on customer feedback. Secondly, risk reporting. If a significant risk was identified, of course it went into the project risk log but could also be underlined in the highlight report.

The advice then is to define how you will assess success when the stakeholder objectives and key messages are identified. The key question is: how do I check/test this? By the way, if you cannot answer the question, it probably means you have not defined the objective/messages well enough yet.

How much stakeholder management do I need to do?

Stakeholder management has the potential to eat up much of a project manager's time. Analysing stakeholders could go into a great deal of detail and take time to find the information you feel you need. The resultant communications can also be costly both in time and resource. Agility suggests you do just enough to achieve your needs. Finding out how much is not science, but I can offer guidelines.

- Stakeholder management should be informed by risk management.
  - Your initial and then ongoing risk assessment may highlight stakeholder-related risks, e.g. opposition, or where stakeholder management and communications form part/all of the mitigating tasks.
- Prioritize your efforts according to your stakeholder analysis, such as:
  - identifying opponents, especially if influential;
  - identifying supporters, especially if influential and prepared to help.
- Scrutinize the project schedule for events where communication would greatly assist, such as:
  - gaining support at project start;
  - achieving a major milestone;
  - gaining engagement when preparing for a stage gate review.
- Beware of people who pretend they are stakeholders but are just wasting your time and effort. These can be recognized from your stakeholder analysis as they have little or no influence or concrete relationship with your project.

Manage or engage with stakeholders?

This may sound philosophical but it is practical and is at the heart of stakeholder management. Some practitioners and APM's BoK 7 maintain that you should engage with stakeholders, whereas management sounds combative. The term engagement as commonly used in management infers collaboration, supportiveness, even mindfulness in some. The connotation of engagement is not military and therefore combative, quite the opposite.

I am *not* criticizing collaboration, supportiveness or mindfulness. In a book about agility, how could I?

But to be clear, the purpose is to get stakeholders, people, to do what you need them to do; to behave in ways you want them to. It is the most people-manipulative tool in the toolbox, some would call it Machiavellian. For me the management of stakeholders sometimes involves engaging with them and sometimes manipulating them. The following table suggests verbs that represent manipulation vs. engagement behaviours.

MANAGE	
Manipulate	**Engage**
listen	listen
direct	persuade
tell	ask
instruct	seek permission
cajole	encourage
isolate	support
exclude	welcome

Figure 5.20: Stakeholder management vs. engagement

My default approach is to seek to bring people with me, to persuade, to encourage and so on. At times however I have felt it necessary to proverbially wield a baseball bat, to manoeuvre an opponent out of the way. Seeking the right way to manage a stakeholder is using agility.

I suggest you find editions of *Yes Minister* to watch – a great satire on British political life and government in the 1980s. Sir Humphrey alas is alive and well, although thankfully there are fewer of them than back then.

Resourcing and talent management

To resource or not to resource, that is the question.

Agility for this subject means managing resources and talent in an organization that supports both business as usual (BAU) and project activity – the new operations. Not just the right capabilities, e.g. subject matter experts, project managers and so on. But also the right level of resource to support anticipated, dare I say, planned BAU *and* project activity.

Example: Opex vs. Capex, and resource planning

Many years ago, I was Head of Customer Projects for a large UK telco. My director and I built a profitable professional services organization. Project based of course. One frustration was not being allowed to recruit as many permanent project professionals for internal policy reasons. I tried to keep to a target of no more than 10% contract project managers. The growth in successful sales pushed that to 40%. While not ideal for customers who wanted permanent not contract people, they also needed their projects delivered.

Problem solved it seems. Alas, the one resource I could not control were the technical specialists, mostly digital telecom engineers. These were seconded from operational (BAU) teams. Not surprisingly there was a limit to the number our professional services directorate were able to borrow and the pressure in operations was to reduce the number as digital systems matured. Operations was not permitted to resource both for their own demand and to resource professional services, due to limits on their Opex budgets. And professional services were not allowed to hire engineers. It limited our customer portfolio growth, although this was partly offset by 1) a number of our project managers were also technically competent, and 2) using contract engineers, often ironically ex-staff, but also from other telcos. Contract staff were paid from a Capex budget, set more in relation to predicted sales and profit margin. Wonderful thing playing with budgets.

From the operations view, a line manager needs to know that they will be able to maintain a level of resource with the right capability that enables their team's performance to at least be maintained, bonuses earned and staff kept happy, or at least kept.

> **Key point:** To support agility in projects, an organization must resource to a level that supports both BAU and project activity.

There are other options, such as subject matter experts who are either ring-fenced for project work, or recruited into the projects resource pool.

Whatever route, this is a major challenge and tightrope for any organization. For instance, if project delivery momentum falters, resource utilization drops like a stone and that is unproductive and expensive.

It follows that if an organizational culture supportive of agility is to be built and sustained, one KPI is its ability to attract *and keep* the right people. This is talent management.

A talent for agility

Speaking of talent management, given that agility is as much behavioural as it is procedural, recruiting for agile behaviours needs to be a part of growing an agile project capability.

In keeping with most writing on agile, there are variations but the nine behaviours below are commonly quoted:

- being collaborative;
- being transparent – open and honest – show me over tell me;
- team over me;
- respecting and listening to others (even if you do not agree with them);
- adaptable, e.g. willing to step outside of comfort zone into another role;
- can do, problem solving;
- willing to ask for help and feedback;
- willing to risk making a mistake;
- accepting of just good enough.

When recruiting and developing people for agile projects, these nine behaviours are as important as technical capability in terms of role profile and selection.

Once an organization and its projects have the talented people needed, they need to be further developed to grow the capability in the organization and of the individuals. But also so that the culture of agility is reinforced.

Training and development of the core project delivery resources is as far as most organizations go. However, for agility to thrive, especially if the target is the new operations (BAU and project activity), then agility must be developed as a core capability.

Example: Airport operations teams
Most operational managers at an airport found themselves involved in projects from time to time. Either as a subject matter expert or even to manage a work package, usually where the scope of the work package related specifically to their team's work. Quite a few operational managers struggled: 1) because they did not have project-related skills which made them inefficient in the role, or, 2) it was incredibly difficult to find the needed time for their 'day job' and project responsibilities. In fact, 2) often arose from 1).

The answer was to train every manager in at least foundation-level project management. Some who were either keen to or likely to work more frequently on projects were provided with additional training and coaching. This successfully mitigated both 1) and 2).

Chapter 6

Adapting project management for agility – Process

The processes discussed in this chapter are common within pretty much any project management method or framework. My purpose is not to go into the detail of techniques such as change control and how they work, but rather how you can use them (in an agile way) in your organization, and what it looks like when you do.

Governance

'Who pays the piper calls the tune.' If I were the piper, I would also want to know the rest of the band are playing the tune well. Governance in a nutshell.

Empowerment is good, but funding organization(s) quite reasonably need to know 1) that their investment is more than likely to return anticipated benefits; 2) that progress is visibly under control; and 3) the way in which things are being done is right.

Applying agility to governance is about applying hands-off leadership to the portfolios, programmes and projects being funded. Which means:

- defining the right level and boundaries of delegated authority, and to whom;
- defining the right level of oversight in the form of Board, reporting, interaction and engagement;
- adapting organizational management and technical standards, e.g. P3M, approvals or performance management of people;
- ensuring that the above are understood;
- enabling decisions which have to be escalated, e.g. change control, to be done rapidly.

That about covers the usual governance scope. If defined and adapted well it can provide the umbrella under which portfolios, programmes and projects are able to get on and deliver. But this is about agility, which really benefits from an even more supportive organization.[12] Other challenges that governance can help with may include:

- the relationship with people resource sources, whether line management, HR for recruitment or procurement for delivery partners;
- IT for equipment;
- facilities management for workspace;
- corporate communications for help with, well, communications.

I am not suggesting governance provides the mechanism for managing their delivery. For example, HR will have their own processes. But remember that agility works best in an organization supportive of projects. Therefore, governance for agility needs to be able to oversee not just the delivery of portfolios, programmes and projects, but also the working of the operational functions that support and enable them – such as the provision of resources.

After all, governance is there so that the sponsor and senior management are comfortable that everybody concerned with projects are visibly making good progress and operating appropriately for success.

Strategy and business planning

In the late 1990s, most MBA courses in the UK barely mentioned projects. Strategic planning, yes, lots of that. Operational business planning related to strategy, lots of that too. How to go about making strategic change happen… tumbleweed. That was more than 20 years ago and MBAs have changed massively. I even lecture on agile project management to MBA students.

Today it is common for strategic planning to include business transformation. Alas, all too commonly, when it comes to implementation, that tumbleweed, the disconnect between operations and projects, remains.

Making the project economy work well requires project-based activity to be an integral part of business planning. There are two main principles.

1. Strategy and plans make provision for project-based activity in parallel with keeping the show on the road (BAU) activity.
2. The business planning and control cycle is adapted for multi-year project activity.

For the first, it is not just about setting budgets for both BAU and projects. For instance, there will need to be a level of resource available to support both BAU and project activity. Unfortunately, it is not quite that simple. When it comes to the pool of project professionals, these can be organized in various ways, but they are there to partake in projects.

But when it comes to technical assistance from operations, there needs to be enough to be seconded to project work, while ensuring the show *is* kept on the road. This is never going to be easy as project resource demand will vary due to numerous factors, such as readiness to start, customer contract delays, lack of sales, project pace and so on. And no line manager likes to carry under-used, costly people. Resourcing and budget setting for the new operations (BAU and projects) needs to go hand in hand.

Agility comes from finding a solution that works for your organization. It can be especially challenging for organizations of modest size.

Example: Security and data products company
The growing company in this example needs both technical and project people for the two types of project it runs: product development and customer implementation. Due to its current size and predicted growth, the CEO realized that ring-fenced product and implementation teams were not affordable. Therefore, while there was a great resource management challenge day to day, a single resource pool was formed and mapped to a single project portfolio.

The portfolio, mapped to strategic goals, held a pipeline of projects:

- proposed product developments or enhancements;
- customer implementations in sales process and pre-contract (i.e. almost there);
- product developments and enhancements being planned ready to go;

- contracted customer implementations being planned;
- underway product developments or enhancements;
- underway customer implementations.

The portfolio position is in any case under constant review. Part of that is now close attention to calendarized resource demand.

In respect of business planning, rolling year budgets are more common than three or five-year plans. Whichever approach an organization uses for business financial planning, it needs to adapt for projects. Multi-year working is not a problem in itself. BAU operations assume that business processes, such as production, marketing, sales, finance, HR and so on, will go from year to year. Allowance for these will be made in the rolling budget (or n-year plan), then allocated to each annual budget.

Project activity starts, proceeds, then stops. This can be tricky even where the project completes within one annual budget, as most operational budgets, cost centres, finance processes, systems and approvals are set up for continuous process.

More challenging is the multi-year project/programme. Some suggestions:

- Consider project-based budgets for project activity that involves multiple functions.
- Consider function-based project budgets for projects within a function.
- Set up the necessary project-centred cost centres.

Approvals

This is an extension of business planning. Projects can arise from anywhere in the organization. Agility as a mindset demands constant focus on the delivery of value. It is true that most in the project profession these days do regard the purpose of projects as delivering not stuff, but value/benefits. This was not always so and is not the universal mindset today. I have interviewed very senior project managers in engineering, especially in oil and mining projects in the field. They rarely if ever get involved in business cases and are focused on delivery within budget. Being agile suggests they must always be shown to be contributing to strategic goals and hence value.

Most should therefore be driven out of strategy and business planning. But this can be at two levels: at the organizational level and within functions empowered to plan for and approve their own projects.

Even if projects are being delivered outside the function, the budgets can be set and approvals made against budget.

If project-related budgets are established, that should make project approval more straightforward. And for agility this needs to be flexible to allow for change. More on this in Chapter 8 under *Managing an agile portfolio*.

Oversight

Once portfolios, programmes and projects are underway it is a matter of oversight (governance) with as light a hand (hands-off) as possible – management by exception. Give much thought to the optimum levels needed for:

- financials oversight;
- reporting;
- standards;
- culture (behaviours);
- support activity from the business.

Planning, monitoring and reporting

Planning in context

Planning, monitoring and reporting are often presented as part of *controlling a project*. Which is fine but carries the bias of process over people, i.e. control through process, which for decades had the impact of ignoring the people aspects. This is not agility.

I prefer *leading a project*, which to me suggests the more effective integration of process (e.g. planning, tracking, risks, change etc.) and people aspects (leadership, teamwork, communication etc.). This is agility.

Separately and together

Planning, monitoring (tracking) and reporting are different project management activities, albeit closely related. So think about what you need from each, as well as how they will work together in your project.

For instance, you might need to delve deeply into a technical plan to procure, prepare and install new air-conditioning equipment in an airport terminal, carried out when the terminal is closed at night. This will enable you to determine the time, dependencies, skills, materials needed, risk and cost.

It may be that you only need to track progress of a specific level of outputs, rather than each component. Therefore, the planning plan may well be more detailed than the monitoring plan.

Reporting may end up being even simpler, i.e. completion of work per overnight when the terminal is closed.

Always keep in mind to do no more than you need to, which is another way of saying *just enough*. And it may seem almost anti-agile, but spending some time planning to plan etc. can save you a great deal of time/effort/cost during a project.

How much planning, tracking and reporting?

Some in the world of agile software development decry the need for up-front planning at all. Let me be clear then. For project agility you need to plan throughout a project and even before in terms of business case development. Planning will occur throughout a project. It will cascade from high-level plans to much more detailed ones, for example, for the next stage in a project.

When I am coaching young project professionals (padawans, if you are a *Star Wars* fan), I commonly have the following conversation.

Padawan: How much planning do I need to do?

Coach: Agility suggests you do *just enough*.

Padawan: How do I find out how much is just enough?

Coach: You should be asking yourself, why am I planning?

Padawan: But you always need to plan.

Coach: True, but understanding what on your project you need to achieve through plans, monitoring and reporting will inform not only how much you need to do but how you will do it.

Padawan: How do I find out?

Coach: Look at the factors both inside your project and outside in the organization.

To apply agility to planning, monitoring and reporting here are ten useful questions you can ask yourself:

- How can I plan to be able to deliver some value as early and often as is practical?
- What is needed for governance, i.e. what does the organization need to see? Are there mandatory governance requirements?
- What level of planning do I need to determine time, cost, dependencies, skills needed, cost and review points?
- Are there experts I could use to aid the plan estimating or plan validation?
- Are there past similar projects that can be used as models and/or for validation?
- What is needed for project quality assurance, e.g. reviews, demonstrations and tests?
- What level of visibility is needed: for me, the team, stakeholders?
- What level of risk is there in delivery?
- What is needed for stakeholders/communication?
- What do I need to enable hands-off leadership?
- What do I need to be able to see delivery trends?

The key factor outside the project is what is needed for governance from the organization. The one constant is money, but let us look at some examples.

Example: Global mining company
The challenge was to introduce a global P3M (project, programme and portfolio management) framework. Operations were organized into geographies and each had considerable autonomy. Efficiency and regulatory drivers called for a move away from the prevalent *not-invented-here* culture. The balancing act was to determine an optimum set of standards the organization required to meet its (i.e. the Board's) needs while preserving autonomy. The solution was a framework which essentially said two things:

- You need to do P3M, and these are the components you are expected to do, but you can adopt whatever local standards you like to do them.
- You also need to adhere to this simple set of requirements for reporting at the portfolio level to the Board, with a consistent content, format and timing.

The core of this was financial reporting against budget. While the heads of each geography had little time for the enterprise PMO, finance could not be ignored. No report, no money. In truth the report was essentially a dashboard of portfolio performance plus financial data.

Example: Energy Technologies Institute (ETI)
The ETI was a public–private partnership between global energy and engineering companies and the UK government. It acted as a conduit between academia, industry and the government to accelerate the development of low-carbon technologies.

Funded by its partners, it ran internal and commissioned external projects. External projects were awarded through competitive tender and usually went to consortia, often a mix of academia and industrials. To avoid micro-managing, key aspects of the governance of external projects included:

- Proof during tender that those bidding had both technical and project management competence, i.e. could do the work and manage it effectively.
- Successful candidates could use whatever project assurance approach they wished so long as they also met and were consistent with optimal ETI governance standards.
- ETI's optimal governance standards focused mostly on visibility of progress against time, cost, quality and risk criteria.
- ETI's governance standards were reflected in contracts and so were mandatory.
- Also mandatory were regular proofs of the effectiveness of project assurance.
- Contracts also allowed for closer inspection (show me) and drill down at need, and otherwise were based on the principle of management by exception.

In other words, there was much agility built into the way in which contracting consortia and organizations were managed. This included hands-off leadership by the ETI programme managers for each technology programme such as offshore wind.

Example: Investment finance programme
The programme delivered a business to customer online investment hub. Part of the programme strategy was for it to be the model for a Europe-wide roll-out. Very detailed planning, costs, risks etc. were done and updated during the programme and actuals were recorded and lessons learned. Far more detail was used than required for the programme's own assurance. But the risk reduction and cost saving to the European programme should have been considerable.

Mandatory vs. flexible

One example where I will spare blushes, partly because it was quite a while ago, concerned a public sector project portfolio. Every *project* had to produce the same monthly report at the same level of detail, irrespective of the size and duration, from a three-month simple project to a four-year programme. The governance percentage overhead varied from minor (programme) to gargantuan (small project). This was to the intense frustration of many project managers, and commonly and ironically led to delivery issues as project managers were forced to take their eye off the delivery ball.

Following a review, changes were made which recognized that one size did not fit all. Among the changes made was that size/scope/complexity/risk criteria were used to determine six categories:

- Small, simple project, 3–6 months.
- Small complicated project, 3–6 months.
- Large simple project, more than 6 months.
- Large complicated project, more than 6 months.
- Delivery programme or small portfolio.
- Change programme.

For each category there were simple but mandatory planning and reporting standards, which reflected frequency and type of milestones, risks and costs. The mandatory components for programmes included stakeholder feedback.

Beyond these mandatory items, projects and programmes used PRINCE2 and MSP and internally developed templates for consistency. But they were able to adapt these standards to the needs of the project or programme.

Using this approach, organizations can ensure consistency at the governance level while not over-burdening projects with levels of management that provide no value to the project or organization.

N.B. I used to say mandatory vs. optional, but that could cause confusion in case optional is interpreted as leaving stuff out. Contrary to incorrect opinion, this is *not* being agile. Agility means considering what does need to be used and how best to do so.

For instance, I know of many oil and gas engineering projects where the project manager has no role in a business case, but still has to manage to a budget.

Mandatory could be another word for just enough. For an organization anyway.

Using tools – how will I plan?

Chapter 7 will provide a more detailed consideration. For now here are ten questions as food for thought.

- What tools are available in my organization?
- How mature is project management in my organization?
- Should I use simple, stand-alone tools such as Excel or enterprise tools?
- What governance or contractual issues are there that determine data use and management?
- Who am I using and sharing data with or providing data to?
- Are they outside my organization? How does that affect tool choice?
- How visible is or can the information be?
- How can I ensure that data is accurate and up to date?
- Is there data available that I can use?
- How can I learn lessons from the data?

Relationship between reporting and communications

Many project managers loathe reporting, but reports are also a communications channel. They are the opportunity for a project manager to give their side of the story or to send a specific message up the line.

A project's communication plan needs to make the relationship clear to show where project reports are fulfilling specific communications objectives. Needless to say, using one technique to fulfil multiple management requirements is an example of agility.

> When establishing a new professional services for a UK telco, I inherited a pool of good project and programme managers. One of their frustrations was the amount of reporting. Not so much the amount of information, but rather that some of them had to produce five project status reports per month: usually similar data, but in different formats, with different emphasis and even at different times in the month. This was to satisfy the needs of different internal and external (customer) stakeholders.
>
> On establishing an enterprise PMO, one deal made with the PMs was to agree a single set of data each had to produce and the format that they would produce once per month to the PMO. The PMO would then issue reports using the data to the various stakeholders. Over time the PMO was able to negotiate standard internal reports and dashboards for the executive. Major customers usually continued with bespoke reports, while most small projects customers accepted a standard report as part of the contract. Especially when project management time was charged!

Commonly, reporting reflects an old principle of *management by exception*. It reflects agility and has been around for decades.

Tell me vs. show me

An important agile behaviour is transparency, which can also be expressed as *show me over tell me*.

This has been much debated as agility requires trust, and if you trust someone to deliver then is 'show me' unnecessary? For me trust is two way, something that must be earned and is at the heart of collaboration. Here are two examples.

Example: Energy Technologies Institute (ETI)
The ETI (mentioned in the previous section) was funded in part by the UK government and several industrials. As a 'greenfield' set-up, all sponsoring parties were closely interested in how operations and governance of externally delivered projects worked. The Board in particular was offered and required considerable detail on both the operating model and then more than just a dashboard of progress. Representatives were invited to observe the physical organization and progress. After six months the scrutiny moved towards management by exception with occasional deep dives, usually by an industrial with a specific interest in one of the programmes, e.g. offshore wind.

Trust earned.

Example: Major software house producing a large government system for a then part of the Department of Work and Pensions
At the time this was a top 20 central government programme. The core capability was an information system being delivered in at least three phases. During the first phase the assurance and openness of information from the supplier was textbook: monthly highlight reports, weekly briefings, regular phone calls. Most RAG statuses were on green or amber with remedial actions reported.

The development used a waterfall life-cycle. DWP subject matter experts and internal business analysts were involved collaboratively with the supplier's team during requirements specification and design. Even the user group received regular communications from the supplier and were consulted on screen design/layouts. As user acceptance testing (UAT) approached, confidence was high on both sides.

Two weeks before user acceptance testing was due to start, a highlight report arrived... late. But just in time for the regular monthly meeting. The supplier's account director joined their programme manager to report that UAT would be 'about' a month late. At the end of a...how can I put this? – deep and meaningful conversation, it was clear that almost six months of reports were – and this is a masterful understatement – inaccurate.

Once heads rolled and the blood cleaned away, the contract was reviewed and amended. The *tell me* based governance was out and *show me* arrived. For phase II, proof of physical progress was demanded from requirements onwards. In addition, a DWP IT team was deployed with the supplier's team to 'look over their shoulder'. A more collaborative approach to working was also put in place where DWP SMEs and some users (with business analyst support) took part in detailed design meetings and reviews, in a scrumish fashion, I now realize.

The closer scrutiny *and* greater access to the customer made dealing with development challenges much easier. After three months and proven green RAGs, the permanent on-site DWP IT team was withdrawn and replaced with weekly visits and demonstrations of working features.

👍 Agility is built on trust, but trust must be mutually earned.

Risk and issue management and problem solving

Project management is about increasing the chance of project success. Or to put it another way, project management is about risk reduction.

Before you start shouting 'hypocrite!' I am not proposing a simple solution. I am not suggesting all you have to do is manage risks. A plan would help, plus some leadership and, well, everything else in the project management toolbox. Now here is a strange thing. Risk is not mentioned in the Agile Manifesto.

Neither is *fail fast*, and yet if you read around agile anything, fail fast is almost ubiquitous. In fact, risk and fail fast go together like climate concern and Sir David Attenborough. Applying agility to projects is to seek to de-risk as quickly as possible, i.e. to *fail fast*. In practice, this means to do the riskiest stuff first. There are two benefits from doing so. Firstly, if you go off track early it is nearly always quicker and cheaper to put things back on track sooner rather than later. Secondly, after the difficult stuff, everything else should be easier. No guarantees, we are talking projects after all.

I spoke to Dr David Hilson (The Risk Doctor) about risks and agility.

Adrian: The idea of failing fast in agile suggests you should do the riskiest stuff first. What is your view?

Dr David Hilson: That's fine but how do you know what the riskiest stuff is at the outset?

Adrian: Well, there are some in the agile project management world that think you do not need to do risk analysis at the beginning of a project, but that risks can be managed during the phases of a project – especially if an iterative life-cycle is used.

Dr David Hilson: It's about reducing *uncertainty that matters*, which should be started as early as possible. It is clear that an initial risk analysis is needed or you may miss key risks that need to be mitigated early in a project.

Adrian: Is there anything else that characterizes agility in risk management?

Dr David Hilson: I am not sure that addressing risks early is especially agile. But being flexible in how you might analyse risks, mitigate and report them is good practice.

Just to complicate things, some project professionals also recognize risks, issues *and problems* (sometimes called impediments) – where problems are little issues that do not require the full panoply of issue management, which is being quite agile really. For example, where a key team member has a child off sick from school for a few days without alternative care, if working from home is a quick and effective solution then it's a problem rapidly dealt with. But a loss of a key team member completely at a critical time with a significant impact on the project – now that is an issue.

N.B. The following applies as much to *issues* as to risks. And to be clear, I happily go along with the APM's definition of risks and issues. For simplicity, you can think of a risk as being something that may occur and has impact, whereas an issue is something that has happened and will have impact, sooner or later. An issue is sometimes called a risk that has happened.

When it comes to applying agility to risk and issue (and problem) management, all the usual risk assessment techniques are available and valid and I will not waste space here explaining them. What I want to do is suggest where agile thinking and behaviours can be applied to the management of risks and issues.

How agility can de-risk a project

Project management exists to provide the greatest chance of project success. Or, to put it another way, to minimize the risk of failure. It is worth revisiting how agility can de-risk projects.

At the organizational level it can ensure clarity of vision and leadership from senior management. And provide a smoother ride such as through resource provision.

Within projects, agility promotes visibility and communication, which reduces misunderstandings and aids collaboration. This itself enables creative, high-performing, self-organizing teams. And the drive for rapid and frequent delivery of outcomes enhances the achievement of value from a project.

Agility and identifying risks and issues

Risks and issues can arise from anywhere, which can make the process of identifying and analysing them daunting. They can arise from:

- the threat of something damaging happening;
- somebody or a group (stakeholders);
- uncertainty – of requirements and/or the best way to meet them;
- the complex or the complicated – see later discussion on this;
- the risk of missed opportunities – with risk of not achieving being applied first to the highest-priority requirements;
- the risk of not doing the project (often useful when compiling a business case).

The PMI also point to *event and non-event risks*, which are what the labels suggest. Then there are *emergent risks*, which come out of nowhere. At worst these might prove Donald Rumsfeld, with his known unknowns and his unknown unknowns, to be a great philosopher. For me agility comes into how a project team, and especially its leadership, is able to react to emergent risks. It is the ability to deal with disruption and change.

How much risk/issue analysis?

Like stakeholder management, this is another area that can tie a project up in knots.

Let's take two ends of the spectrum.

Example 1: A local authority, as part of its green energy and cost-saving strategy policies, is installing solar photo-voltaic panels on the roofs of its buildings. It has decided to adopt an agile approach for the project. Its chosen partner (after tender) also uses agile for its customer projects. Both parties are committed to a collaborative relationship and this is reflected in the contract.

The chosen risk analysis and definitions use a simple 1–3 scale (low, medium, high), combining both risk probability and risk impact to provide an overall risk score. This is deemed sufficient by the authority's own Portfolio Management Office and by the supplier partner.

Example 2: At the other end of the scale is a nuclear plant de-commissioning programme (actually a portfolio of programmes). Here agility is being used not for the entire portfolio, but for some of the research projects that are investigating best ways to meet some of the technical challenges. Agile was decided on as one company involved had already used it successfully to aid creativity in problem solving in another nuclear engineering programme.

However, given the nature of the environment, i.e. nuclear power, there already exist specialist nuclear risk management teams whose people specialize in various technical areas. Agile leadership is being used to ensure they can cross-fertilize ideas. The investment in complex risk management is considerable, but inevitable. In this case, it must be *just enough*.

Some questions you might consider are:

- How critical is this project to the organization's
  - customers;
  - products/services;
  - operations;
  - financial impact (cost or revenue);
  - reputation;
  - people?
- Can people be severely physically impacted if something goes badly wrong?
- Can people be severely psychologically damaged if something goes badly wrong?
- What is the public impact if something goes badly wrong?

If the answer to these portentous questions is 'not much', then probably a simple set of criteria similar to example 1 above is appropriate. Whereas if it is more like the nuclear programme in example 2, then all sorts of risk specialists could be required.

> I have been an assessor of candidates for APM's Registered Project Professionals since almost the beginning. Once I was interviewing a candidate about her approach to risk. She described the team of risk specialists in some quite esoteric disciplines that were available to her. I boggled slightly thinking of most of my projects that simply used impact and probability and the 1-2-3 scoring.

Agility in managing risks and issues

What vehicle should be used for managing risks and issues?

The other way of looking at doing only just enough is not to do more than you need to, and do it in the most appropriate way.

In managing risks and issues there are actions to take. These are recorded, tracked and updated in the risk and issue logs. So usually there would be no need to duplicate this activity in the project plan. But it's amazing how often risk/issue mitigation tasks are doubled up.

> **Key point:** Do not duplicate management.

Unless – and this is where the appropriate bit comes in – the mitigating actions are of a size, scope or complexity so as to make it impractical to try to record and track in the logs. Agility would then suggest translating to an outcome on the project plan with a simple cross-reference in the risk/issue log.

> *Example: Seat-back video aviation programme*
> This programme sought to procure and install a world-class seat-back entertainment system in the airline's fleet. It was assessed that the chosen supplier's system might ultimately not be acceptable. The mitigating action was a project to select a fall-back supplier and produce a fall-back plan. This was clearly a major contingency action and quite unsuited to managing via the risk log, which only cross-referenced to the project in the overall programme plan.

Manage once is the lesson.

What risks/issues to focus on?
Focus on the important risks and issues as indicated by their scores. For risks this will typically be a combination of probability and impact. And for issues a combination of impact and urgency.

👍 Urgency vs. importance.

N.B. Another useful wrinkle is the difference between *urgency* and *importance*. For example, it is important that I work on this business case, but this report for my boss is urgent and needs to be done today. Both concepts drive decision to act. And important things like the business case will change in urgency as the deadline approaches.

What risks/issues are reported?

Agility assumes management by exception and reporting only what is needed by the project and by the organization (including senior management stakeholders). Also assumed is that remedial actions and decisions are taken within the project as far as possible.

But not all actions and decisions can be. Even under agility with empowered self-organizing teams, sometimes escalation is required. When forming a project, a rapid escalation path needs to be agreed within the organization's governance and key organizational stakeholders. For example, it would not be agile to wait for the next monthly project Board meeting to take some decisions such as for urgent change requests or addressing a critical *emergent risk* (unforeseen, coming out of the woodwork).

So too with risk/issue reporting. When considering which risks/issues to report, by default the high-scoring ones will be reported, which also is a form of escalation. I additionally suggest considering risks that require escalation:

- because senior management *need to be aware* of them, and that the project is taking action
  - Example: A key piece of equipment has failed causing delay, which may push a product launch date back. The team has sourced a replacement within the budget and is replanning based on receipt of the new kit.
- because senior management themselves *need to take action*.
  - Example: A key piece of equipment has failed causing delay, which may push a product launch date back. The team has sourced a replacement but only from a currently unauthorized supplier. Procurement has passed basic diligence on the supplier and confirmed this as the only way to preserve our schedule. Sponsor is requested to approve the purchase.

Problem solving

A word about *complex* vs. *complicated*, referenced earlier, which is of particular relevance to agility.

Problem solving is rarely straightforward, and sometimes we do make life hard for ourselves. For me, there are often many right ways to do things, such as problem solving. And of course, there are the wrong ways as well. The trick is to find a right way and avoid the wrong way.

Rick Nason, in his excellent book *It's Not Complicated*,[13] does not claim to have found a magic bullet nor the holy grail of problem solving. But he does suggest at least the starting point for finding the right way to solve problems. And, just as importantly, to avoid the wrong way.

He suggests that problems can be described as *complicated*, or *complex*. This brings me (of course!) to nuclear power stations, which we can decommission – and to scrambled eggs, which we cannot unscramble.

Complicated problems are commonly technical, mechanistic in nature, having set rules, procedures and structures. They are the nuclear power stations. Or the flight paths and holding patterns above, say, Heathrow and Gatwick airports. There are many routes, hundreds of planes (pre-Covid), with seeming chaos in the sky – and yet highly structured (flightpaths) and rigidly controlled (air traffic control). A complicated, even abstractly beautiful, aerial ballet. If you get the chance, search YouTube where the UK National Air Traffic Control (NATS) have posted videos showing 24 hours of flights over the UK.

Complex problems defy highly structured analysis or being defined by a repeatable set of steps or instructions. They are commonly human, i.e. behavioural. They are the scrambled eggs. Trying to unravel why people, whether in my world of projects, or more broadly, act as they do is not rocket science… it's far more difficult than that.

Why is this useful?

If you can define the nature of a problem, that will help you find the right way(s) to deal with it. And prevent you using the wrong problem-solving tool.

Complicated problems tend to be capable of highly structured approaches to problem solving, such as Cause and Effect (sometimes called Fishbone) analysis. For very complicated, multi-faceted technical challenges, you may have come across Six Sigma (see the appendix). It's not just for decommissioning nuclear power stations! You can improve process flows, production lines, and so on through specific measures, structured analysis, step improvements and so on.

Complex problems, i.e. the human ones, do not lend themselves to such highly structured problem solving. Understanding and managing behaviour in projects is certainly easier than trying to unscramble eggs, although not much. And it is not just about behaviour, but also about how people are feeling, and their relationships with others, that can and often does impact what we do and how well we do it.

Not too long ago, these were thought of as the so-called soft aspects with the related soft skills. Even 20 years ago, project management best practice consisted mostly of the hard, the mechanistic techniques, such as planning, risk management, reporting and so on. Reliance on which commonly led to failure. People do not always follow a plan, or set of standards, or even build an Ikea Billy bookcase by following the instructions. Ironically, the so-called soft skills and managing behaviours are well recognized as the hardest of all.

It's a good idea, then, to have a toolbox of problem analysis and problem-solving techniques, aimed at trying to understand and manage pesky humans.

Individual and team performance against planned tasks may be directly measured, but that only tells you the effect, not the cause(s). The human factors mostly have to be indirectly measured.

Example: High staff turnover
A fast-growing professional services company started to see high turnover rates in their project managers. This created problems such as resourcing customer projects and added to costs from using more contract staff. Ultimately, client dissatisfaction and lost contracts were increasing with potential damage to reputation as well.

Once examined, additional symptoms, notably sickness rates among permanent staff, provided indirect evidence. Staff surveys which had been bland and not taken seriously were redesigned to gain specific information about the working environment. Exit interviews were also carried out. The key factors driving resignation were identified as:

- lack of engaged leadership: project managers felt they were left too much on their own, unsupported and only contacted when things were going wrong, not in a good way;
- salaries only keeping pace with inflation while contractors were paid market rates significantly above salary levels;
- contract project managers were not expected by senior management to work as hard and long hours as permanent staff, who often had to support a client out of hours.

The investigation accidentally also discovered that many contract project managers did not return for new projects. That was only discovered when a director had lunch with a friend whose son had worked as a contract project manager.

Sickness and absenteeism rates provide indications, as do staff surveys and dare I say it... managers actually speaking to their people to see how they are. All these can help analyse the problem.

Dealing with the human factors can also be done in both unstructured and semi-structured ways. Good leaders naturally engage with their people and I call this an example of an unstructured approach, albeit vital.

Stakeholder management and planned communications I suggest are semi-structured, if done well, as described in Chapter 5.

But what if the problem is *both* complicated and complex?

Example: Gold medal for change control
During the London 2012 Olympics construction megaprogramme, a major risk was – and let's not mince words – blackmail. There were many major suppliers, hundreds of sub-contractors and thousands of changes. The venues *had* to be finished on time, and the risk of contractors delaying work until change costs were agreed to their liking was very high.

This was both a process (complicated) and behavioural (complex) problem. These were addressed by process adaptation and behavioural manipulation via the contracts. Essentially, all approved changes (and there were thousands) were guaranteed a minimum payment based on a set of criteria. If the supplier/contractor felt they were being underpaid they could appeal. However, the work would progress while the appeal took place in parallel. This enabled work to progress rather than being held up by negotiations... or blackmail.

An approach which, incidentally, demonstrated brilliant agility.

> **Key point:** The nature of a problem can indicate the best approach to solving it.

Change control

This is one of the more challenging areas when adapting agility to project management. The Agile Manifesto states: *Welcome changing requirements, even late in development. Agile processes harness change for the customer's competitive advantage.*

Many practitioners take this to mean change whatever you like when you like. For projects, this is frankly absurd, as projects have to achieve their goal(s) or fail. Changes may occur along the way, but unless they at least achieve or preferably enhance the value gained, those changes are not acceptable, no matter how useful they are to somebody.

The focus is often on the first sentence – *welcome changing requirements*. It reminds me of the mistaken phrase: *money is the root of all evil*. The quote is more correctly: *the love of money is the root of all evil*, which has quite different connotations.

Both sentences provide guidance for agility in project change control.

The ability to accept, even welcome, change to meet customer needs is clearly indicated by the Agile Manifesto.

Agility in change control is characterized by the following points:

- Valid change must maintain or enhance business needs from the project (value).
- Change should be within the overall scope and cost of the project, unless otherwise is strongly justified.
- Any change in requirements must be prioritized.
- Keeping the control process as simple as possible.
- Making the change control process as fast as possible.
- Aim for most change to be decided within the delivery team, exceptionally by the sponsor and rarely escalated beyond.
- Change requests need some simple entry criteria; they cannot simply be 'I want'.
- A high volume of change that deflects resource from delivery indicates problems earlier in the project and may trigger a review.

At the end of the previous section on the complex and the complicated, I gave the Olympics 2012 example, which now works in two sections. How agile of me! Here are two other examples of adapting change control, the first one within quite an agile organizational culture.

Example: Airport project portfolio management
This airport spends more than £200m annually on project-based activity, managed within a prioritized portfolio. A description of how the portfolio is built is described under *Building an agile portfolio* in Chapter 8. Each directorate and its director is accountable for the projects relating to each. Most of the

programmes are cross-directorate and either one director or the chief operating officer (COO), depending on programme scope, is sponsor.

While the budget is allocated to the portfolio, each director is responsible for both costs and benefits of the projects for which they are sponsor. The COO delegates both accountability and budget to sponsors, who are therefore the ultimate change authority.

Directors delegate change authority to project managers unless a change will breach time, cost and quality constraints, including an up to 10% contingency. If change has to be escalated, the project manager and director usually deal with it immediately as they are in an open plan office.

A director is free to slow (i.e. to impact available funding), cancel or change a project in the portfolio under their accountability. Only if they require more budget must they make a case to the weekly meeting of the COO and other directors. The PMO provides any what-if analysis required by project managers, directors or the COO. Most stakeholder engagement concerning change is done directly by the project manager.

There is a great deal of informal communication to smooth the path, aided by generally good relationships, in a collaborative culture created and sustained by the COO.

The second example shows how a programme adapted change control to a high volume of change requests, not within a collaborative culture.

Example: Retail transformation programme
This programme enabled changing most customer engagement from being branch based to online. The marketing project was responsible for defining and producing customer relationship management (CRM) information to support the transformation, much of this as content for the new business to customer website. But also for the use of customer data in the

production of emailed or paper marketing material to be sent to customers.

A challenge emerged for the web development team and project manager. The CRM module entered user testing and much content had been signed off, e.g. for information pages. But both marketing and internal communications kept raising changes not just on content, but also the design of the CRM module. While most of the change requests were ultimately rejected by the process, the project manager was spending 30% of their time dealing with change requests instead of driving delivery.

The programme office, in its role as centre of excellence, worked with the project manager to adapt the change control process to include:

- criteria for change request submission that included the need for business justification;
- an initial filter which reduced by almost 90% the volume of change requests that went to full evaluation.

There was also communication between the programme manager and senior marketing and internal communications to bring them on side, which was critical.

> **Key point:** Project changes must add to or at least preserve project value.

Business case and financial control

Nothing gives a project manager a warm feeling in their gut or a cold knife to their heart at the outset than how well or painfully the business case and financial approval goes.

The good, the bad and the ugly
The good: Investment finance programme. A major strategy delivery programme, the estimated budget was approved in the rolling three-year plan of the organization. The key benefits and

outcomes were identified and owned by the programme's sponsor whose pre-business case had Board and executive-level support. Business case production became mostly a technical exercise to provide more accurate estimates and delivery KPIs.

The bad: A government department which demanded detailed business cases for each of 11 projects in a £24m change programme in addition to the programme's business case. Seven of the projects were enablers with no directly measurable benefits.

The ugly: An engineering company with a four-year organizational transformation programme. Operational governance rules stated all business units had to provide budget requests with justifications annually as part of business planning. Fair enough for business-as-usual operations, not change programmes. The four-year programme had to repeat its business case three times, including full approvals to Board level. This was on top of the programme stage gate and phase reviews which included value for money assessments. In effect, the programme and project managers were deflected from their core role – delivery – for almost six weeks per year.

Agility suggests keeping it as simple as possible for control – just enough financial governance.

- A business case is for the life of a programme or project, but subject to review.
- Value for money reviews should be built into appropriate reviews, e.g. stage gates.
- Projects in a programme are to define costs for the outcomes, *not* have their own business cases.
- The programme maps outcomes to benefits and defines how benefits will be tracked.
- Stand-alone projects map outcomes to benefits and how benefits will be tracked.

While this seems obvious, it is surprising how often some of this is not done, such as actually tracking benefits. Or done in unnecessary detail.

It should be said that justifying project activity is not always done via a business case. A guide is given in the figure below.

Portfolio	Programme	Project in a programme	Stand-alone project
Strategic business plan (part of)	**Programme business case**	**Project brief or project charter**	**Project business case**
Includes: • goals; • outcomes; • justification, e.g. cost-benefit analysis.	Includes: • goals; • outcomes; • justification, e.g. cost-benefit analysis.	Includes: • outcomes; • programme context.	Includes: • goals; • outcomes; • justification, e.g. cost-benefit analysis.

Figure 6.1: Where a business case is and is not required

The business case process

There are two areas of challenge around business cases where agility can assist.

- producing the business case; and especially
- approving the business case.

Agility is about doing just enough, doing it quicker and smarter. Here are some agile pointers.

Producing the business case:

- Confirm the link to strategy and business plans.
- Determine the appetite for risk vs. reward; how far can the project push the boundaries?
- Treat business case build and approval as a mini-project (sometimes not so mini – think HS2).
- It's not a serial process: shape, gain feedback, do more shaping, gain more feedback. In fact, it's iterative.
- Get the right assistance to help shape goals, benefits, the solution, costs, plan and risks, e.g.:
  - lessons/estimates from similar projects;

- - specialists;
  - finance.
- Do initial stakeholder analysis to find who can help review parts/all of the case *and* who you should avoid.
- For a large complicated/complex project or programme, workshops to develop the business case can save time and build common support (yes, this might be iterative).
- The process of producing the case should also be the starting point of approval in terms of bringing key stakeholders on side. Maintain suitable visibility and engagement to ensure you have the full circle, costs, benefits and how you will measure success.
- Ensure that there is a budget available to argue that it should fund the project.

Appetite for risk in a business case

Meredith Landry in his 2013 article 'Risk and reward' discusses this potential upside of risk and how it can be managed though an organization.[14] Given that most projects are about change, testing the sponsoring organization's appetite for risk is an example of agility that should be considered. Projects do seek to minimize uncertainty, but they can also grasp opportunities, e.g. to gain competitive advantage.

Some factors that can indicate the appetite for risk can be seen in Figure 6.2.

Pros	Cons
Risks from not doing the project	Risks from doing the project
• Missed opportunity	• Cost of failure
• Revenue	• Reputational risk
• Market share	• Resources denied to another project
• Damage to competitiveness	
Dare we wait to do this?	Is this the right time?
Embracing risk from change during the project	Risk averse during the project
• Potential to increase benefits	• More certainty over cost and time

Figure 6.2: Assess risk appetite

Approving the business case

This is part of the governance process, often with significant stakeholder *management*.

- Confirm the governance approval process and *who* will actually sign off.
  - N.B. Commonly several formal sign-offs are needed.
- Do stakeholder analysis to find out the best way to get them on side.
- N.B. Approvers being senior people are usually very busy people and difficult to get time with, therefore:
  - Find out who they listen to and how to get them on side; use them to influence.
  - Find out what progress sign-offs there may be along the way:
    - formal: stakeholders who need to review parts of the case and sign them off, e.g. finance;
    - informal: stakeholders who need to review parts of the case to 'give their blessing'. Usually they cannot stop the case but they can hold it up and weaken the 'sell' to the executive if not engaged with.
- Plan your approval outcomes and tasks, including stakeholder management.
  - N.B. Any opposers may need to be manoeuvred in some way.
- If the business case is to be presented for approval such as by the sponsor to the Board, ensure you are advised on how they like such things done. But also remember it is a sales pitch, without hopefully being very *Dragons' Den*.
- Ensure visibility throughout, which helps build trust.
- Ensure your approval plan includes not just gaining budget approval, but authority to spend.

Approval vs. authority

In most organizations there is *budget approval* and there is *authority to spend*; you usually need both. You may have been told there is money set aside in a budget and that you have an approved business case. None of this means you can spend any money on the project. For that you need authority.

I have seen many projects run into problems. For instance, when a project manager is starting the project and recruiting people or procuring contractors or equipment, HR and procurement turn around and ask, what cost centre? The PM goes to finance and asks for a cost centre to be told they have no authority, which they have to get and that is a delay.

Agility means checking how the organization really works in order to smooth the project's path. Also do not forget to estimate how long it will take to babysit the business case through each step of approval, whether formal or informal.

- Who needs to review parts of the business case?
- Who needs to sign off parts of the business case?
- What are the formal review and approval steps?
- What final authority is needed, frequently based on the project cost?
- Who are the influencers to be engaged with?

Budget approval

You may need to ensure that money has been included in the budget even before you start to build a business case, especially for a major programme. Has it been anticipated? In an organization supportive of projects, budgets would be driven from strategic and business planning. It would be the driver for initiating a project.

Within unsupportive organizations, those initiating a project may or may not be the budget holders. Or funding could be from multiple budgets. Agility suggests that to reduce the risk of wasted time, it is wise to ensure there are funds reserved or at least potentially available before much time is wasted on shaping a project and its business case.

This is where the sponsor should be active pre-project and especially pre-programme, even if the figures are high-level estimates +/− n%.

Financial control

During a project, financial management has the nasty habit of tying a project in knots. It is another area where the supportive organization makes life much easier vs. the unsupportive organization, which may delay, damage, even kill the project. Without even trying to!

Figure 6.3 contrasts some characteristics of supportive vs. unsupportive organizations in terms of financial controls.

Supportive	Unsupportive
Strategic plan built from BAU and project activity.	Project activity mostly driven from the middle of an organization.
Business plan financials comprise both BAU and project activity.	Project activity has to find a budget.
Governance adapted to temporary activities, i.e. projects.	Governance unmodified for temporary activities.
Financial reporting guidelines for different size and scope of projects and programmes.	One-size-fits-all financial reporting.
Sponsor accountable for business case with the time and capability to engage with projects.	Sponsor may not exist, or has accountability but no capability to exercise it.

Figure 6.3: Financial controls in a supportive vs. unsupportive environment

Answering the following questions can help avoid these problems:

- What financial oversight reporting is required?
- Who is collecting and providing cost actuals data?
- Have you asked for it?
- Have you got it?
- Where the costs are external, how do you know the costs are correct and/or up to date?
  - They could be mis-assigned to the wrong cost centre, even the wrong ledger.
  - Beware someone laying costs on your project, the sneaky devils.
  - Is operations trying to make your programme pay for a new resource for which you will only use a part, or use temporarily? E.g. equipment or the cost of hiring a new business analyst. This one could lead to an interesting debate.
- Can you match programme reporting timing to financial reporting timing?

Resource management

In Chapter 5, I looked at the people aspects of resource management in terms of agility. This section is more process oriented. Agility in this subject comes from recognizing the challenges and then having the adaptability to deal with them. The table below is really a checklist of common challenges and potential solutions.

Challenge	Description	Potential solutions
Predicting what resources are needed	Resource planning	• Integral part of planning process. • Identify roles and skills. • Skill level and productivity. • Minimum-level skill needed.
Funding resources	Confirming available funding, from which budget(s), and how much is capex or opex (could impact ability to use contractors)?	• Confirm budget source. • Level available for resources. • Capex or opex – may impact ability to recruit contractors.
Sourcing people	Options and channels for resources; map required resource to potential sources, both internal and external. Assess options.	• Relationship with HR and procurement for recruitment and supplier options. • Determine source options (internal/ external). • Map required resource to potential sources. • Match to available funding.
Getting enough people	Ability to gain commitment to sustained suitable resources, with the right capabilities	• Supportive or non-supportive organization? • Establish relationship with owning line managers.

		<ul><li>Negotiate.</li><li>Possibility of mutual support?</li><li>Engage sponsor support.</li></ul>
Getting the right people	Ability to get enough people of the right capabilities and behavioural profile	<ul><li>With the right level of capabilities.</li><li>With suitable behavioural profiles (fit).</li><li>Internal or external?</li><li>Integrating externals into the team culture.</li></ul>
Keeping people	Ability to maintain people's interest in staying with the project	<ul><li>Maintaining personal and team morale.</li><li>Can personal and project needs be aligned?</li><li>Future development?</li></ul>
Onboarding	See self model	<ul><li>Making new entrants part of the team.</li><li>Bringing them up to speed.</li><li>Ensuring they have passes, kit, logins.</li></ul>
Succession planning	Ensuring that if a key person leaves, another or others can fill the gap	<ul><li>Identify people whose loss would have immediate impact.</li><li>Contingency options for replacement.</li><li>Can others step in?</li></ul>
Managing performance	Not just monitoring how well people deliver in their role. But also behavioural aspects.	<ul><li>Monitor their outputs.</li><li>How are they feeling?</li><li>How well are they doing in the team?</li><li>Address performance issues.</li></ul>
Developing people	Helping individuals and the team to grow their capabilities	<ul><li>Integrate with company development scheme.</li><li>Develop in the project.</li></ul>

		• Training and external focus. • Willingness to let them go.

Figure 6.4: Resource management

Looking at the table, one of the repeating themes in this book stands out, that of integration – both inside and outside the project. Resourcing relies on having an integrated plan, on team make-up and dynamics, on finance, on organizational links such as finance, line managers, HR and procurement and on the management of third parties.

Agility arises from the ability to keep these plates spinning.

Third party management and agile contracts

Working with third parties introduces more complexity and complication to how projects operate, both at the project and organizational level. A project may have external people as part of the delivery team and/or as the customer. They have their goals and bring their own culture – behaviours and ways of working. Organizationally, there will be customer–supplier contracts to make. Probably involving the customer organization's legal and finance teams at the least.

In this section I will focus on third parties in a supplier relationship rather than a customer one for two reasons. Firstly, because the stakeholder management and communication section in Chapter 5 has covered aspects of interacting with customers. Secondly, the customer–supplier discussion in this section can be read two ways by you, as either the customer or the supplier. I will however write from the customer's viewpoint.

Agility can be applied to third party management in two ways:

- in the approach used to procure and contract with third parties;
- working with third parties.

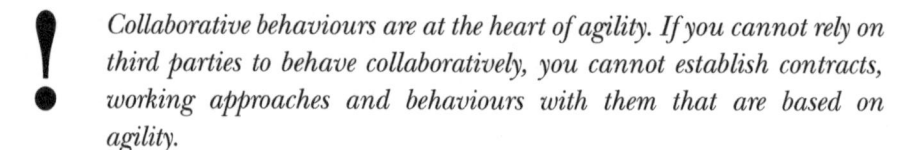

> *Collaborative behaviours are at the heart of agility. If you cannot rely on third parties to behave collaboratively, you cannot establish contracts, working approaches and behaviours with them that are based on agility.*

Procurement

A key skill that good project consultants have is the ability to rapidly find out and understand how the organization they go into works – remember the iceberg. These commonly include:

- who are the key stakeholders, approvers and influencers;
- governance processes – the ones actually in use, and whether they vary around the business;
- finance policies, processes and contacts;
- project standards in use;
- the PMO;
- resourcing sources and contacts;
- procurement approach and contacts.

Internal project managers will usually know at least some of this information. But if they are given a project that involves part of operations they are unfamiliar with, then there is some rapid learning for them too.

Whether an internal, contract or consultant project role, the main goal of procurement is value for money, which is at the core of agility. This does not mean simply taking the cheapest option, which often ends up not the case if the cheapest quote masks future costly change. Any tender must be able to define the criteria for value for money and a fit-for-purpose set of requirements.

> **Key point:** The main goal of project procurement is value for money.

Generally, the procurement options range from:

- tendering for an external organization to deliver the project;
- use of approved suppliers to deliver part of a project or to provide specialist resources;
- use of individual contractors.

In common with this book's approach, I am not going to describe the tender process. Instead, tips and guidance are offered which reflect flexibility and adaptability – the hallmarks of *being agile*.

Ten guidelines for tendering for project delivery:

- Be clear about what outcomes and scope are expected and any constraints such as timescale.
- Be clear about what is expected in the responses to tender.
- Be clear about selection criteria: e.g. technical, finance, governance, resources and ways of working.
- Be clear about what is expected about ways of working.
- Be clear about the kind of delivery partner you are looking for, e.g. collaborative behaviours.
- Be clear about the nature of the team's capability they can muster and whether they can prove it.
- Be clear about what you do not want from them.
- Look for a track record of relevant delivery.
- Look for a track record of working behaviours, e.g. collaborative behaviours.
- Can they prove they can muster the required capabilities?

Again, this may sound obvious but it frequently does not occur. Agility means having a holistic approach.

Example: Lease finance delivery partner selection
A consortium comprising a bank and technology company set out to deliver a business-to-business website for lease finance brokers, who would be able to, while with a client, identify the IT equipment to be leased with costs, conduct company checks, approve the lease deal and order the equipment.

The Director (sponsor) and programme manager, after considering options, decided to build a delivery team comprising both internal resource and an e-commerce development partner. A tender was developed which encompassed all of the above points. Both the sponsor and programme manager were clear on how the programme would operate, its standards and working approach. Two of the three shortlisted finalists, who were called on to present their sales pitch, are noted here.

Company A was one of the top technology consultancies. Their presentation was highly professional and well evidenced apart from one area. When it came to the way in which they would operate and within what framework, they were clear that the client would be better off following their approach. While it had similarities, it differed greatly in the behavioural area; well, it was absent. When challenged the response was that, in effect, they knew best. At that point the sponsor called a halt, thanked them for their work and told them to leave.

Contrast this with another example, the ETI which we met under the section *planning, monitoring and control.*

Example: The Energy Technologies Institute
Although it never used the term agile, from the outset the ETI clearly reflected agility in both its internal operations and how it worked with external delivery organizations and consortia.

Most of its projects were delivered by externals and were selected by tender. The ETI's third party management strategy was based on management by exception:

- use of ETI optimal governance standards – e.g. a standard highlight report (data and format: RAGs for cost, progress milestones, risks/issues, confidence level and overall trend);
- the right and ability for ETI to deep dive;
- planned regular progress meetings based on show me not tell me;
- delivery groups could use whatever project assurance they wished but they had to demonstrate their capability as part of the tender response;
- contract schedules to reflect all the above. For example, contract milestones had to be included in plans and shown in the standard highlight report to ETI.

> It was an example of *hands-off leadership* given contract formality.

Key point: If you cannot adapt to the organization, you cannot have agility.

Ways of working and contracts

Contracts are core to working with third parties. It may seem obvious but you should always have a contract. But after that the role of the contract will vary greatly, largely dependent on the level of trust between customer and supplier, and how well things go.

Sadly, a win–lose culture between customers and suppliers remains common in many sectors, e.g. construction. Although that is changing and there have been some notable leaders for change, such as London Heathrow airport re-construction. There, a more collaborative approach was generated and in which new types of framework contracts played as much a role as behavioural change.

Tendering should not simply be a process of selecting the lowest bid. This often results in costly changes.

For agility, both customers and suppliers must have a common goal: the project's goals. Project success should mean win-win. A customer organization must be clear about what they want from a relationship with suppliers, in terms of outcomes, cost and ways of working. Key to this is the choice of contract and its schedules.

Which contract type?

Earlier I said that procuring and management of third parties is mostly about gaining value for money. Key to this is choosing the right type of contract. On the face of it, this should be simple as there are essentially three types:

- *Time and materials:* paying the supplier at agreed rates for their time and any materials provided.
- *Fixed price:* essentially a given price for a given scope of work.
- *Cost reimbursable:* customer pays the actual cost incurred by the supplier with an additional fee or profit.

Unfortunately, there are variants within these that may either/both muddy the waters or provide a life-belt.

- Fixed price:
    - firm fixed price contract (FFP);
    - fixed price with incentive (FPIP);

            ○ fixed price with economic price adjustment (FP-EPA).
- Cost reimbursable:
    ○ cost plus percentage of cost (CPPC);
    ○ cost plus fixed fee (CPFF);
    ○ cost plus incentive fee (CPIF);
    ○ cost plus award fee (CPAF).

Time and materials often occurs where the outcomes are regular and well understood. Or where there is a framework contract. The government IT system being produced by a software house that we met under *planning, monitoring and control* was an example of this. Unfortunately, due to their poor performance and behaviours leading to a breakdown in trust, the governance aspects of their framework contract we amended for additional 'show me' oversight.

Fixed price and its variants work best for (fairly) predictable outcomes, notably in construction, e.g. in Design and Build projects. There is also a very mixed track record within major government contracts, where the debate over whether an item is a change in requirements or a clarification has been long and expensive.

Variations on cost reimbursable are useful where the outcomes are very uncertain at the outset, e.g. research, feasibility and proof of concept projects. While they risk almost unknown costs, timeboxing and earned value monitoring and some of the variants above can limit exposure.

For agility some guidance therefore is:

- What is the level of risk/uncertainty in the outcomes?
- Is the business environment stable in terms of impact on requirements?
- Is this a development or delivery (roll-out) project?
- Is this part of, or will this become, a regular type of project delivery?
- Is this intended to operate under a framework contract?
- Is this a one-off project?
- Is this a short project or long project/programme?
- Are the potential suppliers well known?
- How trustworthy/reliable are the potential suppliers?
- How secure are the potential suppliers?

Who really carries risk?

All projects carry risk. Contracting with third parties to deliver commonly includes moving risk to the supplier, but at a premium.

> *Example: Having a house built*
> The long-running UK television programme *Grand Designs* has demonstrated many of the pros and cons of different delivery approaches, from complete self-build with the minimum use of 'trades' to contracting out the entire build. Risk is entirely with the self-builder and, theoretically, risk is entirely with the contracted builder – for which they include a premium. In the middle it becomes a little more grey. A main contractor could be contracted to manage any sub-contractors, and so in effect carries the risk for the entire build. Then there is the confusion where the client does some work themselves and directly contracts individual trades, e.g. for plumbing and heating, electrics, flooring and so on.

What happens if problems occur where the cause is difficult to show between the trades, and thus the risk carrier cannot be easily determined? Here, despite what they may have paid for, they will end up with the risk.

But is risk rarely if ever truly transferred from the customer? Looking at the bigger stage of public programmes, such as the fire control programme previously described, while contracts would have ascribed responsibility to third parties, in the end it was the taxpayer who carried the risk to the tune of hundreds of millions.

If you intend for third parties to carry risk and intend to reward that, ensure it is enforceable, and enforced.

> **Key point:** Contracts must show where risk really does lie.

It is possible to mitigate third party risks through agility, such as how change control operated during the London Olympics 2012 construction. To recap, changes if approved were guaranteed a minimum price; the change was incorporated in the work, which continued without interruption. Suppliers could appeal the payment and the appeal took place in parallel with the work and was not allowed to stop its progress.

I believe that the framework contracts under which all Olympics 2012 suppliers operated included this way of working as a schedule to the contract.

Then, too, a contract can be very useful in helping supplier project teams to focus on value delivery.

Example: UK telco professional services organization
One of the behavioural change aspects was to build a mindset among the whole team that value only came when we delivered it to our clients. We were not selling clever digital boxes, cables and whatnot, but capabilities – from which our clients derived value. At the time I had no idea this could be labelled agility, but that is what it was.

Project and programme managers were expected to reflect contract payment points as major milestones in their plans.

In addition, most of our programme directors were mostly selected for their commercial as well as senior delivery experience. For the major accounts, the programme directors were the one role that engaged with the customer from pre-sale through to operations.

We went further to coach the project and programme managers to spot opportunities and value gaps of benefit to the customer which we could provide. This took some time to get used to as the mindset of underbid and then go for costly change was a difficult habit to break for some.

There was another internal aspect which had the side benefit of raising the profile and reputation of the professional services group. A monthly report went from professional services to the Board. Part of the dashboard was invoiceable revenue that month, which showed the value to the organization and of course the value coming from professional services. Previously, only the sales account teams had produced revenue reports. Now the Board was told both billable revenue and actual billed revenue.

Quality management

Total Quality Management (TQM) took off in UK business in the late 1980s and into the early 1990s. Although there were variations, one phrase seemed to sum it up.

Fitness for purpose

TQM drove two key ideas:

- Build products that are fit for purpose.
- Continuous improvement.

Although superseded by the ISO9000 set of quality standards, Lean and Six Sigma, those ideas from TQM still hold value and are built into these later approaches.

In Chapter 2, I suggested that Lean is most applicable for use with continuous, business-as-usual processes, whereas agility is best suited for finite duration and/or one-off activity, i.e. projects. The two ideas from TQM clearly carry through to agility: *just good enough* and *learn and improve*.

Figure 6.5: Saturn V rocket

The label 'quality' can be highly ambiguous, e.g. to the person in the street. Or even highly misleading, as in the world of marketing where 'cheap' and 'quality' seem bound together. For example, compare a Bentley and a BMW Mini. Which is the 'quality' car? The 'quality' car market is defined by Bentley, Rolls-Royce, Mercedes, Ferrari and so on. And yet the Mini is made for its market and, like most modern cars, well made at that. Both a Bentley and a Mini are fit for *their* purpose and are therefore quality products. Also remember the Apollo moon rocket story from the Preface, which bears repeating here.

> There is an apocryphal story that shortly before lift-off for one of the Apollo moon missions, the commander in the lunar module made the following comment to mission control.

'*Here we are sitting on top of the biggest firework ever built, consisting of about 80,000 components ALL built to minimum specification.*'

Why would the manufacturers build the components better than they needed to be – according to the specification? So long as they were built... just good enough.

Applying agility to quality management in projects means:

- Output and outcome quality.
- Meeting the stated needs:
  - against scope of requirements; have enough been delivered?
  - does it do what it should?
- Not being the best it could be, but being good enough.
- The outcomes are useable, supportable and maintainable.
- Quality of delivery:
  - how well did we work?
  - what product reviews, project gates, decision points etc. were used?
  - were they effective?
  - what can we learn?

Adapting for quality

There is no need here to describe the various quality management techniques, e.g. product reviews, project gates and project reviews.

Many organizations have both mandatory standards plus guidance on them.

Agility comes in when applying and adapting to various life-cycles in projects and programmes. And here I will break the 'rule' of this book to delve into an agile managed programme and its agile software development projects. Commonly, the stage gate process assumes a serial life-cycle. How then can that be adapted to iterative life-cycles such as in Scrum and programmes with multiple phases?

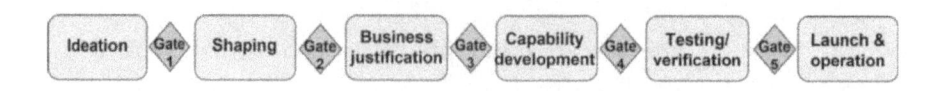

Ideation → Gate 1 → Shaping → Gate 2 → Business justification → Gate 3 → Capability development → Gate 4 → Testing/verification → Gate 5 → Launch & operation

Figure 6.6: Stage gate process

Example: Supermarket retail point-of-sale (PoS) programme
In this programme, all projects had serial life-cycles except for the project to configure and develop some bespoke PoS software. The supermarket's standard stage gate process was similar to the set of stage gates above. Part of the agility adaptation for the programme modified the standard programme gates to:

Feasibility (G) → Business case (G) → Procurement (G) → Design (G) → Development (G) Roll-out

- Design could not complete until an integrated solution design for hardware, software and roll-out strategy had all been aligned.
- In the end there were three development phases running in staggered overlap over a period of 14 months. Interim gates were planned every three months with a major gate at the end of Phase 1 to decide on roll-out readiness for the first operational versions of hardware and software.

The PoS software project had three phases running in staggered overlap, each of which had these internal stage gates:

Backlog (G) → Development (G) → Integration & release test (G) → Pilot (G)

- The development stage was up to six months and consisted of fortnightly sprints:
  - fortnightly sprint reviews and retrospectives;
  - progress data, e.g. size of bow wave (requirements that should have been developed but have not been) fed into monthly reports;
  - quarterly input to the programme interim stage gates mentioned above.
- The gate at the end of the pilot indicated readiness for roll-out.

This approach integrated Scrum with an adaptation of standard governance and use of sprint data held in Jira. The result was very little additional overhead was needed to comply with stage gate programme assurance or organizational governance.

Quality of project management

Quality management should also be applied to how a project is being managed. Lip service is often paid to this, but reviews, such as stage gates, should not only look at progress made and the next stage. They should also ask, 'how well are we managing?' Stop, start, continue could be a useful approach. The basic questions being: What should we start doing? What should we stop doing? And what should we continue doing?

Roles and responsibilities

Applying agility to projects, programmes and portfolios has very little impact on roles and responsibilities. *All* the existing roles remain. The only new role is that of agile (project management) coach.

What is changed, or rather added, are the behavioural responsibilities:

- Agility in leadership roles means that nurturing tends to be more important. A role profile for emotional intelligence.
- The assurance of collaborative behaviours in the team.

This does not mean that affiliative, empathetic leadership is all that should be deployed. As described under leadership, the greatest demonstration of leadership agility is to be able to adapt leadership style to the project, team, person or even the moment.

For agility to be effective, there are changes in roles and responsibility out in the organizational landscape:

- Those in sponsor roles have the role as part of their day job, with time planned for the role and performance measured.
- In fact, all senior roles should require engagement with projects as part of their day job.
- Leadership roles to include the coaching of people and teams.
- Line managers should have responsibilities for providing resources, e.g. SMEs, but the quid pro quo is they have to be supported, e.g. with back up resource so that operations are not compromised.
- Potentially, all operational managers will find project involvement a core skill.

Chapter 7

Adapting project management for agility – Tools and AI

The journey to AI

At home we have Dobby. Dobby is a 'robot' vacuum cleaner. Set it to auto and it scans the room (somehow, I have *no* idea how) before seemingly setting off in a random direction. A little later it has finished and found its way back to its charging station, all on its own!

Dobby is the kind of tech I really love because it means I do not have to do work I do not enjoy, and gives me more time for cooking, gardening, playing drums (badly) and even chatting with my partner.

Figure 7.1: Tools supporting project management

Technology should be one of the greatest, most powerful enablers to agility in projects: automating information gathering, synthesis, distribution, communication and even badgering people to complete tasks for projects. Remember this wordcloud (Figure 7.1) from Chapter 5?

In the last few years, AI (artificial intelligence) has been getting much attention in the project world. There is no doubt that technology to support projects has come a long way during my 30-year career. I have even designed some of it.

In the early 1990s, while working for BT (British Telecom as was), I had the privilege of seeing some of the work of their research laboratories at Martlesham Heath near Ipswich in Suffolk. One technology in R&D became the broadband we know today. High-speed data over copper phone lines and then fibre-optical cables.

I also remember the frustrations of my customer-facing project managers using 56kbps dial-up modems in hotel rooms to submit reports and place equipment orders.

By the early 2000s, broadband and the almost exponential increase in processing power (Moore's Law) led to an explosion of P3M (project, programme, portfolio) tools. This was and remains a double-edged sword.

There are many fine software tools available, from the enterprise level to small project planning apps. This is good... and bad, for the same reason: that there are so many.

Spoilt for choice – choosing software tools

The software choice dilemma is a telling example of how project success is dependent on the project and its organizational environment.

- Should there be an enterprise PM tool that everybody uses?
- Should my project be able to choose?

There is no simple answer but I can offer some pointers which certainly reflect agility, especially in terms of delivery value and doing just enough.

Remember these ten questions from Chapter 6 under *Planning, monitoring and reporting*?

- What tools are available in my organization?

- How mature is project management in my organization?
- Should I use simple, stand-alone tools such as Excel or enterprise tools?
- What governance or contractual issues are there that determine data use and management?
- Who am I using and sharing data with, or providing data to?
- Are they outside my organization; how does that affect tool choice?
- How visible is or can the information be?
- How can I ensure that data is accurate and up to date?
- Is there data available that I can use?
- How can I learn lessons from the data?

Tools and project management maturity

I have had to procure and implement project software several times. I have even designed P3M tools back in the 1990s. My golden rule is: *never buy a tool until you have Level three management maturity*. Level three being *Defined*, which means the processes (templates, workflows, decision points etc.) and behaviours are embedded and pretty stable.

The key reason for this is that tools, especially enterprise-level ones, require configuration of workflows, decision points, interfaces and templates, templates, templates. The less mature these are, the more you will have to reconfigure, which is very expensive. Plus it can make an enterprise PMO look like an idiot if they are constantly having to change templates, reports and especially executive dashboards.

There are just two caveats. Firstly, if you have a brand-new project organization, a true greenfield site, you can use the best practice built into good enterprise tools as your standards.

Secondly, if you are doing pretty much stand-alone projects, choose what you like as you are less likely to be causing anyone difficulty.

> *As discussed a few times in this book, projects are not well integrated into many organizations. So even if there is quite a mature project capability supported by good tools, it is likely that those tools are not – cannot – be integrated into the business-as-usual management information systems, such as finance and resourcing or even the corporate risk register. This lack of operational linkage only serves to perpetuate organization–project separation.*

Single or multiple tools?

There has been a long search for the holy grail of project management tools. And many very excellent tools have claimed and do claim to provide it.

I am not going to say unequivocally that there is no holy grail yet. It is more complicated than that. Unfortunately, I think there are two key stumbling blocks to agility from tools:

- the relationship between projects and their organizational landscape (see Chapters 2 and 4);
- the many different types of project there may be: IT enabled, non-IT change, and so on.

Tools allow us to automate process, which means the manipulation of data. In projects there are essentially two sets of data:

- information about the outputs/products being delivered, such as information relating to requirements, design, testing, training, user products;
- management information used for project control, such as plans, risks, stakeholder map, budget planned vs. actuals.

And as we like to muddy the waters, sometimes data sits in both categories. And here I am again about to go off-piste and use a software example, albeit software product development. I do know of at least two agile engineering product development companies that use the same approach.

Example: Wrangu GDPR app customer implementation
Wrangu produce risk, security and privacy management software, such as for GDPR compliance (General Data Protection Regulations). With this commercial client, Wrangu and the client both use the Jira tool. Jira enables development to be planned, tracked and released, and is based on user stories. This means it is both a development and a management tool. Both parties also use Microsoft Project to plan and as the basis of upwards reporting. Areas of the project such as training, implementation planning and cutover to live operation are

done using MS Project. Software development is limited to sprint start and end milestones.

This approach was agreed as it matched the support tool capabilities of both organizations and resulted in the lowest project control overhead.

I have observed organizations successfully using integrated project, programme and portfolio management (P3M) enterprise tools. We came pretty close in Cable & Wireless a good few years ago.

- Project managers remotely used a standard front end for schedule, budget, risk, output completeness and stakeholder satisfaction data.
- This fed into the PM3 tool, which produced a number of configured reports for internal use and clients, including a senior management dashboard. Trends could be analysed and deep dives done if needed. Bespoke analysis and reports also could be done.

Alas, it took a long time to wean some directors away from pretty, visually stunning but time-consuming and completely non-smart PowerPoint reports. The opposite of agility.

I have also observed a financial organization that spent half a million pounds on an enterprise P3M tool more suited to construction. And they were at about Level 2 management maturity (repeating but *not* embedded approach). The configuration and support bill for the first year of operation was £100k. Not good value for money and therefore not agile. The unsuitable tool was abandoned before further good money was thrown after bad money. I could have saved them the bad.

Tools, reporting and communication

Finally, tools do not just save time, but also perform a duplicate function. Remember that reporting and communication are closely related.

Keeping stakeholders informed, or reminded, can be greatly aided by the right tools:

- progress report configured with data of interest to them;

- prompts in their email or text messaging;
- internal social media for giving and sharing views and updates.

And of course, virtual meeting tools. During the Covid-19 pandemic, most of us probably had a love–hate relationship with these.

Overall, remember that tools are just that, tools. They should be our servants not our masters.

Key point: People over process *and* tools.

Chapter 8

Adapting project management for agility – Portfolios and programmes

Throughout the book, to avoid the constant reference to the wordy phrase *projects (programmes and portfolios)*, I have more simply used the term projects. Although most of the descriptions of agility apply to projects, programmes and portfolios.

In this section I will highlight what agility looks like when applied to programme and then portfolio management. But I will focus on aspects not covered or only lightly so elsewhere.

Agility and programme management

From the outset in the early 1990s, programme management has always been about creating an umbrella under which its projects can thrive. Programmes look both outward, into the organizational landscape for funding and so on and inward to manage its projects. It is a simplification, but for the most part a programme's projects should not have to look outward, e.g. to obtain resources, as the programme does that. This enables the projects to focus on delivery, i.e. to thrive.

N.B. Stand-alone projects also manage both outwards and inwards. In some organizations, portfolio management provides some of the umbrella functions for such projects.

Facing outwards – the programme and organization

An early challenge for the agile programme manager mobilizing a programme is to understand whether it is within a *supportive* or *non-supportive* organization. In the former, obtaining resources, the operation of governance and so on should be straightforward, as programmes and projects form part of the operational model.

If the programme is to operate in a non-supportive organization, then pretty much everything has to be negotiated or even fought for. The risk to the programme from the organization is much higher. It leads to additional engagement, adaptation, negotiation, cajoling, calling in favours and so on. The resultant management overhead is far higher, mobilization takes longer and is more costly.

What this often leads to is the project manager as hero. Able to overcome all odds, find resources from somewhere, find a workaround or a way to circumvent a process. While this may be agility by a creative project manager, it is not agility for the organization. For example, using a personal network to grab some good engineering design resource for a project may help it, but seriously damage others who already had that engineer scheduled for them. If a delayed project is of greater urgency or value than the hero's one, that project manager has done no favours for the organization.

Agility should not about one person, but the team and organization.

Key point: Is your organization supportive or non-supportive?

Having run or rescued change programmes in multiple industries, it used to surprise me that people in an organization often did not know how their organization works in practice. This is usually critical for understanding how a project will be delivered. Remember the iceberg metaphor for organizational culture? Sponsors and portfolio managers who are disconnected from the operations real world may end up driving for unachievable schedules.

Example: Nano-technology company
This is a company which makes and maintains the machines that make microchips. This story goes back a few years but would be highly relevant in the early 2020s and the global chip shortage. A key challenge was to produce machines quickly enough or to repair them for demanding customers, the larger superconductor manufacturers.

If agility is largely about satisfying the customer, then this company was very far from agility. Their customers constantly complained of late delivery despite a great product. All work was projectized to try to manage throughput more effectively. There were new machine projects and maintenance projects.

There were many issues relating to a huge difference between what sales promised to customers vs. what could be physically delivered. Investigation discovered one key factor, one key person, the resource manager, who allocated resources to projects. The key inputs they were provided with were the new sales delivery schedule and the maintenance contract Service Level Agreements (SLAs) which contained turnaround timescales. Neither of these was realistic, on top of which, every director with a complaining customer would seek to change the work allocations.

The resource manager was forced to frequently re-allocate resources between projects. The projects had no say in this and adjusted their schedules. The impossibility of pleasing any customer was maintained.

The fix was not simple and required more honesty during both pre-sale and contract management. While far from easy, in conjunction with the resource manager, achievable project dates were negotiated with customers.

Agility could even be built into the delivery and maintenance portfolios to some extent, driven by customer demand. Such as speeding up work on a machine in maintenance by delaying a new machine for that customer.

🕐 **Key point:** Know how your organization really works.

Facing inwards

I have already written about hands-off leadership and adapting leadership style (Chapter 3).

How the sponsor and programme manager work together is well defined. But in practice I have found that a programnme manager often has to mould and guide operationally busy sponsors. This might include finding ways to support them in their role and to negotiate the time the sponsor commits to the programme. Is this facing inwards, yes, as it is important that the sponsor is seen to be part of the programme team, rather than be out in the organization looking in.

However the relationship is worked out, both roles need to work to sell the project's vision, and create and sustain energy within the programme team. The programme manager's influence is usually apparent more on a day-to-day basis than the sponsor, who can add further gravitas at key moments.

Never forget the role of gravitas in projects.

Project manager to programme manager?
N.B. Another aspect of vision. Back in the day, project managers were commonly selected for their ability to focus on project delivery no matter what was going on around them, come hell or high water as the saying goes. A behavioural trait of any leadership role in projects, programmes and portfolios remains the drive to deliver – being outcome and value oriented. What I found in BT engineering, however, was that many project managers did not make it as programme managers precisely because they were almost blinkered in their come hell or high water behaviours. They could not do the helicopter vision needed for a programme manager. And worse, they could not adapt.

Key point: Agility means the ability to adapt.

Programme shaping

Agility seeks to introduce a particular characteristic during shaping, to seek ways to deliver outcomes and hence value as early and as often as possible. Dependencies and the complexity of outcomes could make this a challenge, but it should be a shaping goal.

In terms of the shape and structure of a programme, generally there are only two 'givens' for how it works. Firstly, that a programme consists of a set of related projects, all focused on delivering specific value. That is not far away from APM or PMI definitions. Secondly, that the programme will have to operate within organizational standards. Governance always, and usually internal project/programme management standards.

This means that the programme manager, sponsor and team need to, and are free to, determine the most appropriate structure and adapt the standards. Here the mixture of art and 'science' opens the door for agility.

It is true that often the nature of the programme's outcomes will inform or even dictate the projects, such as the supermarket retail programme where the projects inevitably were:

- procurement;
- hardware configuration;
- software configuration;
- roll-out.

Even within this structure there were options. Would there be a single phase of procurement, then hardware and software configuration in parallel and then roll-out? The answer was no. After procurement it went like this (see Figure 8.1).

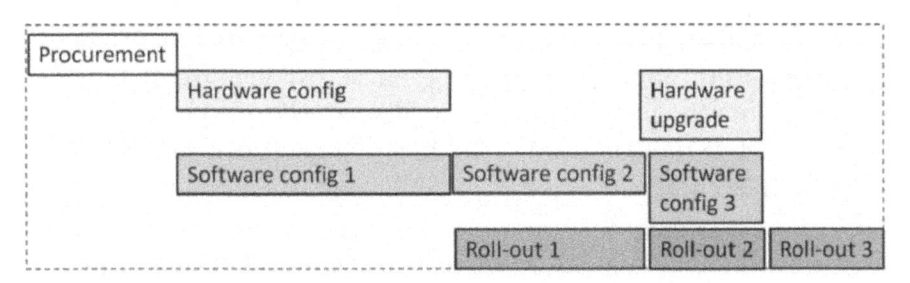

Figure 8.1: The phases of the PoS programme

Projects too had their structure, which was subject to change. In the case of software configuration phase 1, the initial structure of two Scrum teams working in parallel had to be increased to three about half-way through following a time vs. cost/scope debate and decision. In the end it was decided to bring forward functional scope planned for a later phase with its associated budget. This followed a change request from marketing. The project and programme manager made the decision and notified the sponsor.

Programme delivery

I will say little here as both people and process agility have been covered in the first two parts of this chapter.

Suffice to say that agility can also come from having the space to step outside the existing assurance operating in a programme/project. Perhaps to focus on one or more specific aspects. You would have to be confident that the assurance as a whole is 'on the green'. If not, you would risk taking your eye off the ball. In any case, you should only do so for a finite period. It is an old example, provides a good lesson and is remembered fondly.

Example: BT PhONEday
We have met BT PhONEday before in Chapter 6. It added a single digit to every phone number in the UK to massively increase the available telephone numbers – still ok more than 25 years on.

In the last three to four months before going live, delivery was proceeding well. Network changes were ready and were being thoroughly field tested. Communications penetration survey results were good. Not quite green across the programme board, but the programme seemed like a well-tuned engine or the Chelsea football team in full flow (I apologize if you follow any other club).

Given this, the programme top team spent the last three to four months daily asking… what could go wrong? The management focus shifted to risk, though not at the expense of the rest of programme assurance. It was simply that all the rest was ticking along, giving the top team the space to ensure that nothing would stop the programme delivering at midnight on 16 August 1995, on time and with no significant issues.

There is a post-script which again shows the benefits of good senior management engagement. One month after PhONEday, there was a close-out party for the team. BT's group managing director came and gave one of the best, most enjoyable speeches I have heard from a leader. He said:

'Do you know what I have heard about PhONEday in the last month?… [pause]… Absolutely nothing… well done!'

Agility and portfolio management

Portfolio management maturity varies greatly. Commonly, the low value end consists of a list of programmes and projects, with some progress tracking and reporting. The top end is typically characterized by a managed portfolio, driven by business planning prioritization and budgeting with both dashboard and deep-dive monitoring and reporting and resource planning. Plus the assurance and support of the use of project, programme and portfolio management framework and standards.

Agility in portfolio management reflects a point made before. That success depends on what goes on inside a project, or in this case a portfolio, and what is happening in the organizational hinterland. So I will look at:

- applying agility to managing the portfolio itself;
- applying agility to how the portfolio, its programmes and projects interact with the organization.

Organizational agility and portfolio management

In Chapter 2, I described the idea of the project economy and the Organizational Project Management Model. The former reflects the increasing projectization of even business-as-usual work, and the need for organizations whose operations are supportive of projects.

Use of portfolio management is about as close to organizational project management and being supportive of projects as most organizations get.

There are organizations that go further and have portfolios driven (more or less) by business strategy, which is closer to the PMI version of organizational project management.

The opposite of this is a portfolio driven from within the business. Some would claim that this is agility in action, the business defining projects it needs to deliver value. It shows local authority, responding to local need, for its local 'customers'. Lots of agile boxes being ticked.

It may also lead to the situation I found in a mobile phone company several years ago. They had just completed a major strategy revision. I was asked to look at their project portfolio and found about

400 IT programmes and projects. Only 12 programmes were directly referenced in the strategy. Following a portfolio review and removal of duplicates, non-aligned projects, pet projects and some merging, the new portfolio had 22 programmes and 171 projects – all with auditable links to strategy.

Business units being given authority and budgets for projects as part of their operations is a great starting point for agility. But only if the focus is and remains on value to the organization. Portfolio build should be both top down and bottom up. Not just value for the business unit, or indeed a director/VP within it.

> **Key point:** An agile portfolio delivers value to the whole organization.

Permanent portfolios

In 2012 a PMI article, 'PMOs under pressure',[15] stated that the lifespan of a PMO (and by extension portfolio management) was two years. At the time I felt that was about right. It is about the time it takes for project, programme, portfolio management capability to reach Level 3 maturity – where everything is embedded and performance is pretty good.

Unfortunately, that is when what I sometimes call *Y2K syndrome* rears its head. To explain, here is a short conversation I had in March 2000 at a conference.

> *Adrian:* How did Y2K go for you at midnight Dec 31st?
>
> *IT director:* Thankfully no significant problems.
>
> *Adrian:* You must be pretty pleased.
>
> *IT director:* Well yes but all that money, I'm getting loads of pressure from the CFO as to whether it was justified. Why did we do it?
>
> *Adrian:* Well, do you think you would have a job if you didn't?
>
> Pause

IT director: No.

Adrian: Well, if the CFO asks again, tell him it is so that he still has a job too.

I have had directors say to me that the PMO was no longer needed as things were going so well. And this in an organization where they had already gone through two cycles of portfolio management and PMO, get to Level 3 capability maturity and good project performance, then ditch the capability and watch their project performance plummet. What is that saying? Fool me once shame on you, fool me twice shame on me?

Run ahead 20 years and there is much talk, and at the least, huge anecdotal evidence for the projectization of work, even of business-as-usual activity. Often linked to financial accounting years. Lots of projects are always one year long. But there are also many variations of this. This runs on top of the seemingly ever-increasing pace of change, needing the umbrella of projects and programmes to deliver it.

The argument for permanent enterprise portfolio management and associated PMOs grows ever stronger. Does this sound familiar? Permanent means business as usual, projects, programmes and portfolio management as part of operations. A key driver for organizational project management.

Then we need to look at drivers outside the organization, especially competition, or just value for money in the cash-strapped public sector.

All this adds up to the need for slick, responsive, adaptable, flexible, value-focused portfolio management, i.e. portfolio management agility.

Portfolios and the business planning cycle

At the beginning of this section, I mentioned top-down and bottom-up portfolio build. Whatever happens, a portfolio has to be driven by strategy. There may be some looser ties where innovation and/or research and development are breaking new ground, which may or may not work. My thanks to David Hancock who rightly reminded me of this during an event in November 2021.

Being driven mostly by strategy, portfolio build and management need to become a part of an organization's business planning cycle. Given that most are both annual and multi-year, the fact that projects and certainly programmes run across financial years should 'just' be an adjustment to budget forecasting, approval and management, as discussed in Chapter 4.

The result would be something like:

- non-project-based business-as-usual activity repeats year to year, e.g. manufacturing, marketing or finance;
- project-based business-as-usual activity repeats year to year, e.g. regional-based customer support, or IT operations (e.g. DevOps);
- project-based change activity runs both within a year (short projects) and multi-year (longer ones and programmes).

Project-based activity may make it easier to delegate authority to owners of parts of the budget, e.g. an IT operations manager: here is money to run our IT, spend it wisely. Flippant and simplistic I know but it makes the point that agility can be applied to organizational governance.

For non-agile organizations they have to manage the mismatch between BAU governance and governance for *change*.

Building an agile portfolio

Bringing agility to a portfolio management means:

- ensuring it clearly maps initiatives to value (strategy);
- using clear criteria that is as simple as practicable;
- ensuring the portfolio is prioritized and regularly re-evaluated;
- ensuring initiatives can be costed with validity;
- that each initiative is assessed at least at high level for
  - the horizon it is needed within;
  - risk (both of doing and not doing);
  - opportunity;
  - deliverability;
- being able to change the portfolio driven by business need as simply as possible.

You might say that the above characteristics are how any project portfolio should operate. All I can say is that I wish that were the case.

N.B. I have so far referred to initiatives for the portfolio rather than projects. This is from experience and observation that if an initiative is defined initially, it may translate into a programme or a project. It allows more flexibility early in portfolio build.

There are various ways that strategy can be modelled and linked both upwards to vision and mission and downwards to tactical level, e.g. initiatives and projects. Balanced scorecard is one; the VMOST model (Vision, Mission, Objectives, Strategy, Tactics), which I will use, is another.

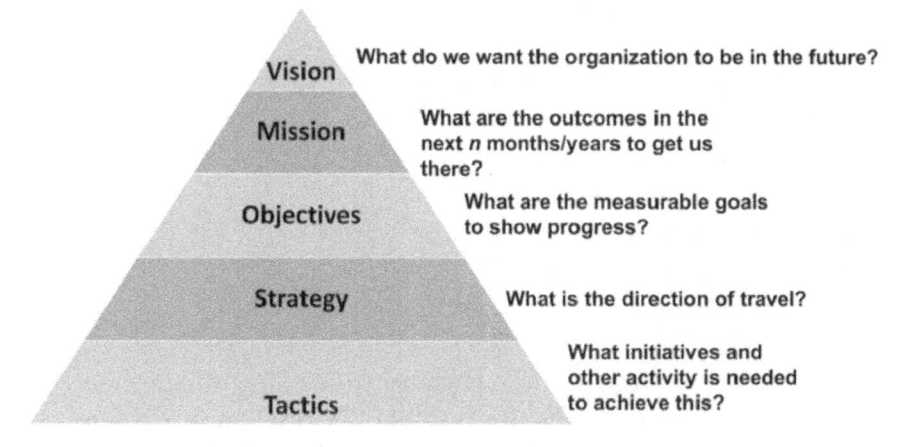

Vision — What do we want the organization to be in the future?

Mission — What are the outcomes in the next *n* months/years to get us there?

Objectives — What are the measurable goals to show progress?

Strategy — What is the direction of travel?

Tactics — What initiatives and other activity is needed to achieve this?

Figure 8.2: VMOST model

N.B. The VMOST model can also be applied for programme and project definition.

In preparation for this book, I looked into my archives for things I had written or presented about the structure of a portfolio and one thing struck me. Bearing in mind some of this material dates back more than 20 years, what struck me was the similarity of a portfolio to a *backlog* used in Scrum agile software development. The scope may be different but you start with a set of requirements, prioritize them and then map those approved for delivery into sprints for Scrum development and programmes/projects for your portfolio.

Using the VMOST model we get:

1. **Vision:** provides the shape of the future.
2. **Mission:** what changes to the organization and/or capabilities do we need to make over a specific planning horizon, e.g. 12–18 months?

3. **Objectives:** the goals we are going to use to test whether we have achieved the mission.
4. **Strategy:** the rules and criteria we will use to build the portfolio that reflect the mission.
5. **Tactics:** the initiatives to be evaluated.

Example: Airport portfolio build

This airport invested about £200m per year on project-based work. I will focus on the Strategy and Tactical levels.

The *Strategy* consisted of five strands:

- regulatory compliance;
- revenue opportunity;
- cost reduction;
- service improvement;
- maintaining a stable operation.

These became the key criteria against which any initiative was assessed for inclusion in the portfolio. A brief proposal was required for each (proto business case) to include:

- criteria met;
- outcomes to be produced, mapped to criteria;
- measurable goals for the outcomes;
- outline cost;
- key risks, including risk of not doing;
- planning horizon;
- deliverability statement.

Although the budget was not set at this time it was estimated. In truth, the COO knew within £20m the likely available budget. Therefore, the portfolio could be built against an expected budget range.

The next step was to prioritize each initiative. Weightings were applied to each of the five criteria so that each initiative could be placed in a weighted list. At this point many initiatives had the same weighted score. The goal was to use MoSCoW to arrive at the final portfolio.

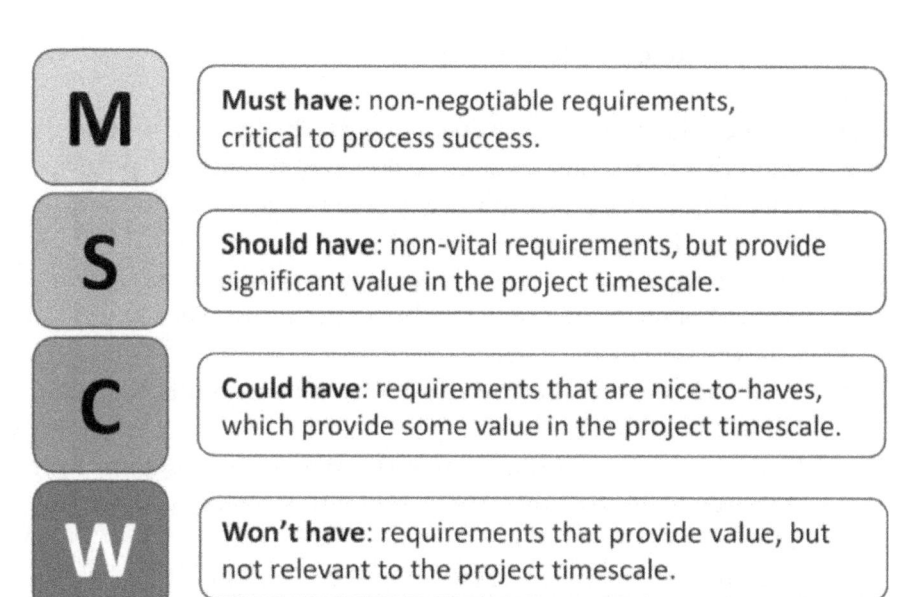

M — **Must have**: non-negotiable requirements, critical to process success.

S — **Should have**: non-vital requirements, but provide significant value in the project timescale.

C — **Could have**: requirements that are nice-to-haves, which provide some value in the project timescale.

W — **Won't have**: requirements that provide value, but not relevant to the project timescale.

Figure 8.3: MoSCoW prioritization

The next stage was for each initiative's sponsor – the relevant operational director – to use factors such the outcomes, e.g. level of increased revenue or decreased cost, to refine the weighted scores. One of the directors, who would end up with the greatest number of (smaller) projects, wanted more granularity in their criteria to help their prioritization. This helped them and impacted nobody else so this additional bit of agility was approved.

The final stage was negotiation. Initiatives to meet regulatory compliance were automatically approved. After that the criteria and evidence significantly *informed* the eventual portfolio. Crucially, however, the decisions were made by the operational directors and COO.

The result was a MoSCoW-prioritized portfolio of initiatives where the must haves and should haves were mapped to the estimated budget. This is also when the initiatives were translated into programmes and projects.

When the final budget was known, in effect those above the available budget line were approved and those below the line went into the could haves.

Ten agile portfolio build tips:

- Define selection and prioritization criteria that link to strategy.
- Keep those criteria as simple as possible, not just for portfolio build but also for portfolio change management, but be prepared to flex them where needed.
- Ensure initiative/project value is always identified and expressed in terms that match at least one of the criteria.
- Cost the initiative/project.
- Risk and deliverability are also useful for informing selection, but are not critical.
- Consider key stakeholder interests. Where two projects have the same or close priority score, stakeholder needs can become a factor.
- Consider having at least two rounds of selection.
- Choose a suitable prioritization approach, which will also inform the structure of your portfolio.
- Ensure the prioritized list is matched to budget.
- The evidence presented significantly informs but does not drive selection decisions.

In the end it must be people who decide the portfolio, not for pet projects, but because the data can only take you so far.

Managing an agile portfolio

There are two aspects to this:

- monitoring the portfolio, taking remedial action where needed and reporting;
- managing changes to the portfolio.

Portfolio assurance

Agility would suggest simplicity, demonstrating value, visibly meeting the customer need and being flexible. With this in mind, here are ten tips to help build agility into the control of the portfolio:

- Meet the needs both of organizational governance and visible control of the portfolio's programmes and projects.

- Track not just outcomes but also their benefits.
- Manage by exception but have the ability to deep dive.
- Have the ability to prove progress, i.e. show me as well as tell me.
- One size does not fit all, e.g. small, simple projects should not have the same overhead as a programme.
- Have consistency of data and reporting and ensure data is accurate and up to date.
- Avoid doing things more than once as far as possible.
- Integrate reporting with stakeholder communications.
- Do not just stand back; be ready to provide guidance and assistance to programmes and projects.
- Do just enough.

Two other aspects can greatly assist, which are the use of a PMO and automation.

High-value PMOs do a great deal more than collate data and report. Just as a drummer is the backbone of a rock band, a PMO should be the backbone of the project delivery capability. More below.

If the project delivery capability has achieved Level 3, this is when a common P3 tool may add considerable value and save a great deal of time, offering the following features:

- a common data repository able to ensure data consistency;
- the capability to submit, view, edit and delete P3 data;
- the ability to roll-up data, e.g. for reports and dashboards;
- the capability to deep dive into P3 data by exception;
- configurable dashboards and reports for different stakeholders;
- analysis of trends in performance;
- capturing a range of project data: schedule, risk, finance, completeness, actions;
- visually presenting data and analysis;
- interacting with users, e.g. reminders of pending actions via email or SMS text message.

Portfolio change management

Change happens. Helmuth von Moltke, Chief of Staff of the Prussian army before World War 1, said that 'no battle plan survives first contact with the enemy'. Or as some wag put it, 'no business plan survives first contact with customers'.

The Agile Manifesto says embrace change and I agree, but again with my caveat that in the projects space, any change must at least maintain or preferably enhance value.

Project and programme change control can be difficult enough. All change disrupts, which is why impact assessment is done. Changes to the portfolio may impact not just projects yet to be started, but also projects underway, which may delay, defer, de-scope or even stop them. Bear in mind that impacted underway projects have sunk costs. Not the least to say a disgruntled stakeholder somewhere.

Talking of stakeholders, just because you have managed to build an evidenced-based prioritized portfolio, beware the attempt to sneak in pet projects. Also beware of troublesome stakeholders who repeatedly submit a project that has not made the cut, in the hope of wearing down the governance. *'Oh let's put it in just to shut them up.'* An already approved project would probably suffer. In addition to the evidence, a good way of dealing with this is to tell them to speak to the sponsors of the projects that may be damaged partially or fatally, perhaps through diverted resources. It could become a good spectator sport.

I sound negative but I do not mean to be. Valid change will maintain or, even better, enhance the portfolio's value delivery. And new projects may emerge from anywhere.

Requests to change the portfolio also disrupts the effective oversight of the portfolio. So portfolio change management must be efficient and enable a balance between disruption and delivery. The following should aid agility in the management of the portfolio:

- Establish a regular reporting and review cycle, which should be part of an information flow that matches both organizational governance cycles, e.g. month end financials, and project/programme reporting.
- Have a portfolio change control process that enables both a standard path (which should be as nimble as possible) and a fast path for changes assessed as urgent.
- Have default portfolio change criteria that match the original project selection and prioritization. To enter portfolio change management, a request must provide this evidence.
- When change arises, suggest a two-stage approach. An initial triage can:
    - test validity and weed out the obviously weak cases; or, for those that pass this test;

- assess urgency, should the change be assessed via the fast or standard path.
• Have clear approval paths, preferably within the team that manages and owns the portfolio.

Example: A business school's operational project portfolio
This business school had two portfolios, one relating to the functioning of the business school and changes to the buildings and infrastructure; the other related to project-based academic activity. This example concerns the former, although a single PMO supported both portfolios.

The operational groups were organized as buildings, services, IT and grounds. A prioritized portfolio matched to that year's budget and the rolling three-year business plan was in operation. In the second quarter, two potential projects emerged. The portfolio was compartmented into projects and budget for each group and owned by the head of each group.

Firstly, following a clarification from the EU Commission, there was a change to regulations issued by the UK government (can you guess when this was?) requiring changes to how student personal data was held. A modest change but required within six months. The PMO recognizing a regulatory change escalated it immediately to the the Chief Information Officer, who, after a brief review by one of the senior business analysts, approved two changes in the portfolio: a delay to a small project which would carry it into the following year, and the inclusion of the regulatory change.

Then a delivery lorry skidded on ice and badly damaged a security booth. This impacted all four groups. A new building was needed, with all services including IT, and a temporary detour in the grounds to allow for re-building. The building's head of group immediately canvassed her colleagues who agreed hire of a temporary portacabin while the main rebuild project, which included planning permission, was shaped and formally walked through the portfolio change process. It was decided to fund the portacabin and services from the operational budget's contingency fund as Opex.

In both cases, 'the letter of the law' was followed, supported by the PMO who ensured a documented audit and decision trail. But informal communications between key stakeholders hastened decisions. This reflected a flexible culture with considerable trust between peers.

Agility and the PMO

There is a range of PMO scope, as mentioned above, from mere data gatherer and report producer, to being the backbone of project delivery capability. The greater their scope, the greater the potential value to be gained. They cannot be accountable for the portfolio, that is for a sponsor-level role, but high-value PMOs are characterized by the following:

- PMO as manager and guardian of the portfolio and the associated budget(s).
- PMO as guardian of benefits management from the portfolio.
- PMO as information hub, not just reports but analysis and advisor on trends and remedial actions when needed.
- PMO as hub interface with operational functions, e.g.
    - for resource management via HR, line groups (internal resource) and procurement (external);
    - for financial control with finance, governance and audit.
- PMO as Centre of Excellence:
    - owner of P3 standards, not as guardian of rigidity of practice, but the opposite;
    - advisers on adaptation of P3 standards, guardian of the mandatory, coach of the flexible;
    - co-ordinator of a community of practice and peer reviews;
    - coach and channel for mentoring;
    - co-ordinating link to external development and professional bodies.

Looking at the above, it is no wonder there are inevitable tensions in the operation of a PMO. On the one hand, they have almost a policing function. On the other, they are the advisers, the hand-holders. With inevitable trust issues. There are various ways to flex this.

- A clear vision and purpose for the PMO within the P3 capability.
- A well-communicated vision.
- A culture of agility that promotes flexible working within some mandatory standards, meaning the PMO can help to streamline project assurance while maintaining the mandatory governance.
- Clear and well-communicated customer–supplier expectations. It's about quid pro quo as collaborative behaviour:
  - project managers keep project information up to date;
  - PMO can use it to create up to 90% of reports, leaving some free text for additional messages useful for a project manager to send up the line.
- PMO in two parts: the governance and assurance side and the centre of excellence side.
- Rotation of PMO people between the two groups.
- Rotation of project and programme managers through the PMO for a few months.
- PMO co-ordinating an active community of practice.

N.B. To reiterate, a PMO can be *responsible* for the portfolio and its management, and for assurance and supporting use of delivery standards and frameworks. But a PMO cannot be *accountable*, as this is for senior management.

Remembering that the biggest danger to a PMO and portfolio management is its success, it is important to not just deliver value to the organization but to be seen to do so. I remember doing a presentation to a director's conference entitled *What have the Romans ever done for us?* – with an, I hoped obvious and amusing, allusion to the Monty Python film *Life of Brian*. While it raised a few eyebrows, it opened quite a few eyes to what a PMO could deliver if allowed to thrive. Hmmm, there is that word again.

Chapter 9

Becoming agile... at projects

How agile are you prepared to be?

One of the themes running through this book are the two spaces that impact project success: the space inside the project and the space around it – the organizational landscape.

To date, the most common initiative to improve project delivery success (and hence value) has been to introduce portfolio, programme and project management frameworks, standards and associated PMO, taking them to at least Level 3 capability maturity. This needs considerable investment and there is plenty of evidence that this does deliver some value.

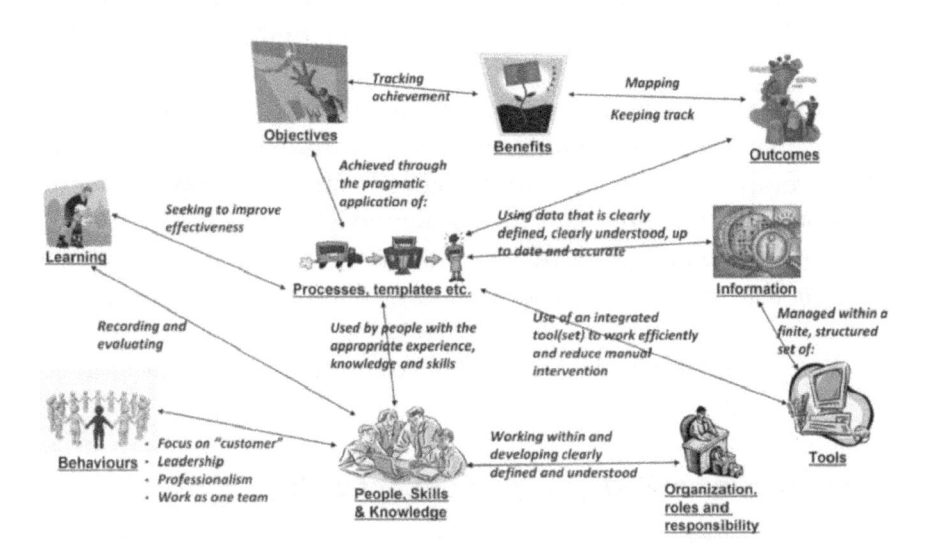

Figure 9.1: Integrated model for project agility

That raises the big question, which comes in two parts. ***How much value do you want to gain from agility and what are you willing to invest?*** By invest, I of course mean funding, but I also mean human capital, as moving to agility requires a change of mindset.

A high-level integrated model that I hope informs your thinking is shown in Figure 9.1.

I have often been asked: *can I be a bit agile?* The answer is yes, *but*. And the 'buts' are:

- If you limit the ambition and the investment you limit the value.
- If you do too little or it is too fragmented, you may cause more harm than good.

Be clear, it is a hard road:

- There are costs both in funding and political capital.
- Opposition from powerful stakeholders.
- Loss of some talented people who will not come on the journey and leave.
- Business-as-usual challenges that will always get in the way.
- The sheer complexity and complication of the change.

Yes, it is a difficult sell, but it really should not be. I ask you to revisit Chapter 1 and what it said both about the value from being agile *and* the risks to competitiveness from not being agile. And I ask you to remember another part of President John F Kennedy's moon speech at Rice University, 12 September 1962: '*We choose to go to the moon in this decade and do the other things, not because they are easy, but because they are hard.*'

Key point: Have a clear vision for how far you are prepared to go with agility.

Vision, mission and strategy for project agility

> *Ikea: Our vision is to create a better everyday life for many people – for customers, but also for our co-workers and the people who work at our suppliers.*

Although it comes from retail, Ikea's vision statement offers a useful influence for organizational project agility. Its first part sets out what it wants for its customers, while the remainder is about its people and third parties.

Another organization that should influence your vision for agility is the Association for Project Management. Their vision is: *…a world in which all projects succeed with project management as a life skill for all.*

If, or should I say when, you go on your own project agility journey, look at your organization's current vision to see if it needs to change, especially if projects are, or will become, core to delivering value to your customers: the projectization of your organization.

When you form a programme to transform to project agility, that too will need a vision. Even if it is as straightforward as:

> *'To improve our project delivery agility, so we can deliver greater value to our customers more successfully and faster.'*

Under the VMOST model, the Mission provides the shape of outcomes over time. This is one reason why I like to use a maturity model as the basis of a change programme. Maturity models show you what each stage looks like when achieved. Which means you can set outcomes against timescales with measurable goals. Such as:

- in 6 months we will achieve Level 2 maturity, which looks like…
- in 15 months we will achieve Level 3 maturity, which looks like…
- in 24 months we will achieve Level 4 maturity, which looks like…

Strategy is where you need to start to link *Business* and *Operating* models. Parts of the Strategy will relate to how your organization will create value for its customers and for the company. They will develop into the business model. Other parts will be for organization strategy and lead to the operating model. The operating model has to show how the business model will be achieved.

Winning the C-suite and other stakeholders

This is where the journey starts. How does it start? With a CEO socializing with peers and the talk moves to agility? Or reading an article such as 'The project economy has arrived',[16] in the *Harvard Business Review?* An approach from someone in the organization they might listen to? Even from a bad experience with agility and then a conversation with a competent specialist.

However it starts, the move to agility in projects is going nowhere unless the C level believe in it. The bottom line for them is going to be, well, the bottom line. If a commercial organization, the question is: will there be profit in doing this? If in the public sector it will probably be more about value for money. So here is reminder of the benefits that ultimately result in value from agility.

less
learning   risk   trusted
            delivery
rapid outcomes
control   adaptability
customer value faster
satisfaction high quality
transparency

Figure 9.2: Value from agile

But there are other considerations as well, some of them very human:

- Organizational factors:
  - pros
    - major shareholder or stakeholder pressure to change;
    - we are losing competitiveness, e.g. to disruptors, we must do something.
  - cons
    - major shareholder or stakeholder reaction to costly change;
    - we have a stable, mature operation – why rock the boat?

- Personal factors:
  - pros
    - this will increase my authority and influence;
    - what benefits me benefits my organization.
  - cons
    - will it benefit me (e.g. CEO, CFO, CTO etc.)?
    - why should I stick my neck out?
    - I think the company is operating well;
    - projects? what projects?

In the end, the benefits of project agility are *not* about projects, but about how the organization, and the people who run it, gain value. That is how it should be sold.

👍 Find the value triggers that will push the C level buttons.

Avoiding the pitfalls

It is too easy to make mistakes with agility, as we saw in Chapter 1, such as mistaking Scrum software development for project management. These eight tips for avoiding the pitfalls of becoming agile should help:

- The senior leadership must *understand agility*, head and heart, and actively lead with *stakeholders* so that they *buy into agile working*.
- Leadership is setting out to establish an agile friendly organization.
- Define your goals for project agility.
- Determine how far agile needs to penetrate.
- Define *who needs to be agile* and help them be so.
- Define how business processes need to change.
- Define what *technology* can help, and/or needs to *change*.
- *Be an agile leader*, e.g. live the agile values, communicate the vision and goals for project agility and the outcomes to achieve them.

Above all, agility in projects can only be led and sustained successfully from the top.

Not throwing the baby out with the bathwater

My partner and I live not that far from Yeovil in Somerset (UK). Although it retains some of its older parts, it is one of many towns in the UK that had its heart ripped out in the 1960s. I am not against new; in fact, I am a fan of modernism – albeit about 100 years old itself. But I agree with my partner, a retired architect, that if you are going to do new, do it good. He would also say there is nothing wrong with re-inventing older styles, with better materials and for energy efficiency. The sadness comes from demolishing something just to build something new. Even more sad when that new is just bad.

The same is true of organizational change. In his 2004 book *Change Without Pain*,[17] Eric Abrahamson described the folly he termed *creative destruction*. Discarding without proper thought, or too much change too quickly before benefits can be realized, is destructive. If the discarding is also people, especially the older, most capable, but most costly people, then suddenly an organization has not only got rid of key knowledge and experience, but has also paid to do so. In other words, do not throw the baby out with the bathwater.

> **Key point:** Build on what works well.

Instead, Abrahamson proposed *creative recombination*, where elements could be recombined and built on, instead of scrapped and replaced. He identified five *recombinants*, labelling them:

- *people* – employees;
- *networks* – relations between people in the organization;
- *culture* – values, norms, behaviours, informal systems;
- *processes* – business as usual, or project activity, formal systems and the technology that supports them;
- *structure* – organization components, lines of communication, reporting.

If you think back to the iceberg picture of organizational culture, all of the elements within that map to one of the five recombinants. They also map to my simpler set comprising People, Process and Tools, which I will return to shortly.

Examples of creative recombination for our journey towards agility in projects could include:

- Use existing work structures but make them more flexible.
- Make existing governance more flexible.
- If there is already Level 3 project capability maturity, grow it to Level 4 for agility.

I would observe that if your capability is already at Level 3, many characteristics of agility will already be emerging so let them develop.

An agile project management maturity model

Consistent with Abrahamson's creative recombination, one of my favourite change tools, the Capability Management Maturity Model (CMMM), can be adapted to describe what organizational project agility can look like at the various stages of maturity.

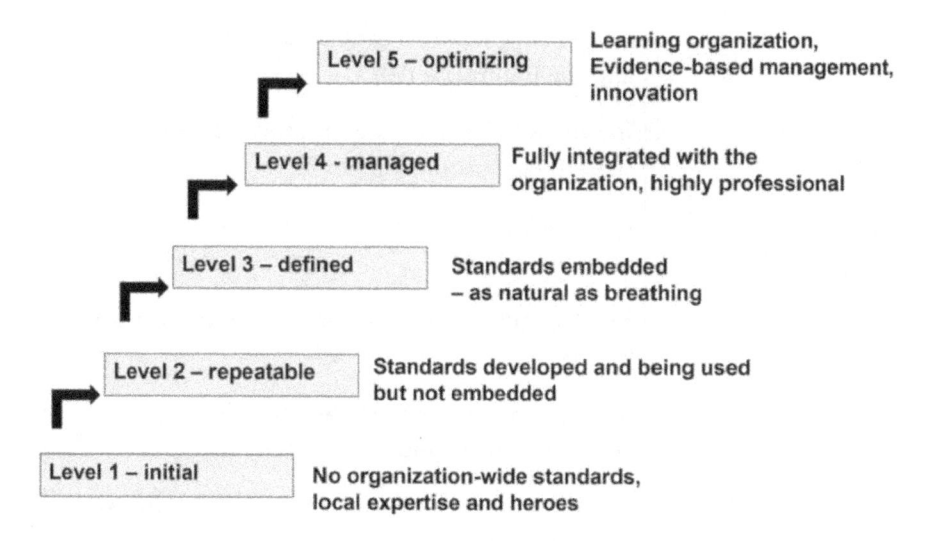

Level 5 – optimizing: Learning organization, Evidence-based management, innovation

Level 4 - managed: Fully integrated with the organization, highly professional

Level 3 – defined: Standards embedded – as natural as breathing

Level 2 – repeatable: Standards developed and being used but not embedded

Level 1 – initial: No organization-wide standards, local expertise and heroes

Figure 9.3: Capability Management Maturity Model

Such models started out to be able to assess processes, given that agility is accepted as being about 50/50 process and people, with technology being critical to supporting processes. Therefore, maturity model for agility in projects, at both project and organizational levels, can be structured using People, Process and Tools.

N.B. Abrahamson's five recombinants have been included within the triumvirate.

184 Agile Beyond IT

In this book, the full Capability Maturity Model for project agility in organizations is not shown. I have to keep some commercial secrets. But most of the components are shown in the three tables below.

Agile PMMM group	Component
People	
Structure	Board actively leading and sustaining, e.g. project delivery representation as Board member or Non-Executive Director.
	Board-led change programme for project agility led by Board member as sponsor.
	Enterprise PMO as control body.
	Enterprise PMO as centre of excellence.
	Interactions between projects and programmes and the Enterprise PMO.
	Interactions between the Enterprise PMO and shared/support functions.
	Locations of project-based activity (including remote working).
	The suppliers needed to support the project-based working.
	Definitions of empowerment (decision rights, accountabilities) and its flexibility.
	Rapid escalation structure (e.g. for risks, issues, change control).
Networks	Resourcing between line management and project leaders.
	Enterprise PMO and shared/support functions (e.g. finance, HR, procurement, legal, internal audit, corporate communications).
	Enterprise PMO as centre of excellence and the project's community of practice.
	Enterprise PMO and externals (trainers, coaches, auditors, business schools, professional bodies).

Agile PMMM group	Component
	Project's community of practice.
	Sponsors' peer group.
	Sponsors and business-as-usual leadership and line management.
	Sponsors and the Board.
	Sponsors and directors of shared/support functions.
	Sponsors and customer executives.
	Sponsors and third party executives.
Knowledge/skills/ experience	Project management skills/knowledge part of core management development.
	Hands-off and adaptive leadership training and coaching.
	Collaborative and other team-type development training and coaching.
	Professional development path in projects.
	Flexible development path mixing project and business-as-usual leadership.
	Training in project, programme and portfolio management framework.
	Coaching for P3.
	Mentoring scheme for project leaders.
	Organizational project agility coaching for executives.
	Remote working leadership training and coaching.
	Remote working training.
	Role profiles and descriptions reflecting agile working.

Agile PMMM group	Component
Behaviours	Establishment of an agile mindset at all levels engaged with projects.
	Team focus on value for the customer demonstrated.
	Hands-off as default leadership style.
	Adaptive leadership as target capability.
	Collaborative, self-organizing teams as default.
	Ability to adapt behaviours to customer, project and team requirements.
	Teams and team members are not afraid to fail.
	Trust and openness demonstrated.
	Proactive, can-do attitude demonstrated at all levels.
	Appropriate and well-judged use of assumed authority.
	Willingness to share knowledge and experience demonstrated.

Figure 9.4: Agile CMMM: People

Agile PMMM group	Component
Process	
Core processes	Core organizational governance processes in relation to project-based working (strategic planning, business planning, finance, procurement, legal, security).
	Core project, programme and portfolio management processes, templates, workflows and decision points, e.g. gates (P3 framework).
	Guidance on adaptation of P3 framework to project size/complexity/risk.
	Definition of mandatory (optimal) governance and assurance standards.

Agile PMMM group	Component
	Guidance on mandatory (optimal) governance and assurance standards.
	Performance measurement processes and reporting.
	Resourcing plans that support both business-as-usual and project working.
	Flexibility on resourcing between internal, outsourced and contractors, e.g. to fill gaps.
	Integrated control and reporting schedule (organizational, governance, portfolio, programme and project).
	Learning and sharing process and practice.
Support processes	The processes needed to support the core processes, such as HR, procurement, legal, security, internal audit and corporate communications.
	Resource procurement (permanent, contract).
	Service procurement and contracts.
	Guidance on obtaining and using support/shared services.
Policies and standards	Business model mapped to (target) operating model comprising business-as-usual and project-based working.
	Organizational values reflecting agility, e.g. empowerment, self-organization and collaboration.
	Statement of the 'offer' that will attract and retain people to the agile organization.
	Policy and guidance on risk appetite in projects.
	Policy and guidance on informal and assumed authority.
	Flexible procurement policy to support agile project-based working.

Agile PMMM group	Component
	Framework supplier agreements that allow for agile working.
	Supplier contracts and schedules to support collaboration and other types of working.
	Remote working policy.
	Security and privacy policy and standards.

Figure 9.5: Agile CMMM: Process

Agile PMMM group	Component
Tools	Plan for tool selection and usage in relation to process and working practice maturity.
	The information systems needed to support core and support processes.
	The equipment and technology needed to execute core and support processes.
	Remote working tools and guidance on use.
	Internal social media tools and guidance on use.
	Collaboration tools and guidance on use.
	Organization cloud storage and guidance on use.
	Integration of tools to support project working and other management systems.
	Configuration of tools to support P3 and related processes.

Figure 9.6: Agile CMMM: Tools

In keeping with agility, the model is there to be adapted to individual organizations.

Roadmap to agility

This is a major organizational change programme and should be treated as such.

The people and technology outcomes are likely to be the most challenging. Mindset and behavioural change are core; therefore, stakeholder management and communications will be critical. Remember the saying thought to be attributed to Drucker: *culture eats strategy for breakfast*. So seek to deliberately build the culture you need – or risk getting one you did not intend. An early risk analysis will inform this, as well as tips contained in this book. Suggest using the iceberg model to determine what needs to change, *and*, remembering Abrahamson, what can be built on.

The technology challenges will be, well, technical. But also probably a procurement conundrum. Which P3 supporting tools? How can they be integrated? What changes do I need to make to existing MI?

Process adaptation at project, programme and portfolio level is more about usage than changing the processes themselves. Organizational-level processes should not be difficult *if* the will and the drive from senior management is there.

The programme's strategy will probably need to contain:

- stakeholder management strategy;
- technology strategy;
- procurement strategy;
- integration and implementation strategy;
- process strategy.

I termed this section 'Roadmap to agility' because I see this as a journey and a roadmap seems appropriate. The roadmap should be a staged plan, based on the agile CMMM and its stage outcomes, which is very handy.

Each stage then will have a minimum of four parallel streams. It is therefore suggested that each stream becomes a multi-phased project:

- people;
- process;
- tools;
- stakeholder management and communications.

Build agility into your programme as far as you can. Even with good risk and stakeholder management, problems, risks and issues will crawl out of the woodwork. Empower the delivery team as far as possible, especially the sponsor, so that they can bring authority rapidly if needed. This is why a Board-level sponsor is suggested.

Although this must be a top-down-led initiative, part of the iceberg analysis at the outset needs to identify the local expertise, good practice and ways of working that should be incorporated and built on. There are four good reasons for this:

- not throwing the baby out with the bathwater;
- reducing the cost of change by reducing the amount of change to be done;
- it allows the programme to be both bottom up as well as top down; which,
- helps empower people through encouraging their ownership of and engagement with the ways of working.

Key point: Above all, this does not happen by accident.

Good luck on your journey.

Chapter 10

Conclusions

In my Introduction I said that the drivers for this book and for agility in projects were two-fold:

- Organizations that fail to embrace agility broadly are likely to suffer, perhaps in market share and certainly in performance.
- That agility can be the framework in which a step change in project performance and hence value delivery can be achieved.

During the book, a theme I repeated was that project success... or failure... depended on what happened not just inside a project, but what was going on outside in its organizational hinterland.

Given the evidence from organizations that have embraced agility to considerable benefit, agility is compelling. Therefore, it seems a no brainer to apply agility to how organizations deliver their projects.

This is the first conclusion.

Chapter 3 unfortunately showed that any journey towards project agility is fraught with pitfalls and misinformation. But that can be avoided; forewarned is forearmed.

This is the second conclusion.

The main body of the book showed what project management looks like when agility is applied. And as people have – rightly – pointed out, it looks like good project management.

This is the third conclusion.

If you or your organization want to drive towards consistently good, even great, project management performance, do what high-performing project organizations do: have an integrated approach, where the organization itself is supportive of projects, such as shown in the Organizational Project Management Framework (OrgPM Framework™).

This is the fourth conclusion.

The journey to high performance is itself not easy and needs a roadmap, such as a capability management maturity model with a set of defined components, which could be grouped under the headings: People, Process, Tools.

This is the fifth conclusion.

Putting all this together, a framework for project agility could be a model for growing and sustaining a high-performing project capability for individuals. And if combined with something like the Org-PMFramework™, for the whole organization too. And as this will be transformative for your business, it should be managed via a business transformation programme.

This is the final conclusion.

Board members and project professionals, the ball is in your court.

Appendix

Learn more about lean vs. agile

In Chapter 2, I proposed that while lean and agile seem interchangeable as terms, this can cause confusion and that they can and should be kept separate.

Lean arose from repeating operational business process, whereas agile is more associated with finite activity, often project based. This distinction should be used for clarity.

It would have clouded the issue to properly explain the lean process in Chapter 2 so here is some additional explanation with examples for those who are interested.

First a rule of thumb, which I will then explain.

- Use lean for continuous process, e.g. a production line.
- Use agile for finite process, e.g. project activity.

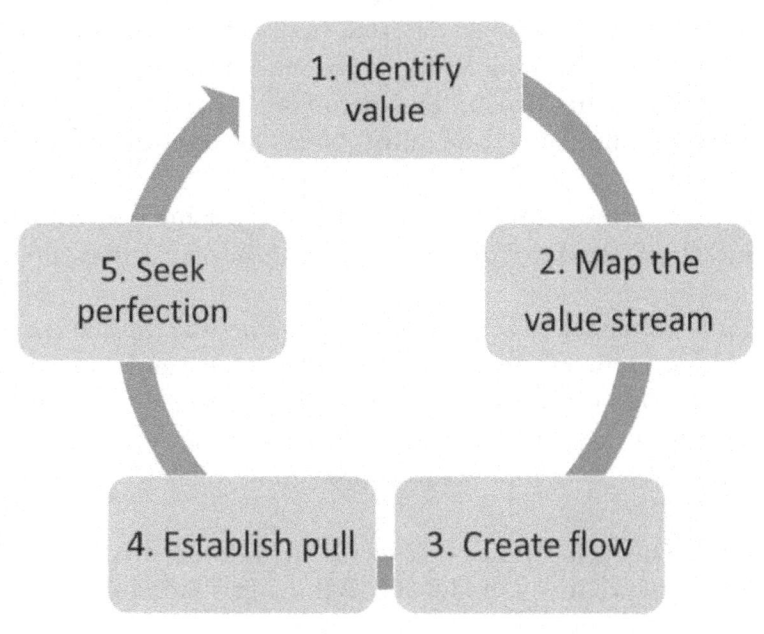

Figure A.1: Lean process flow

Although arguably much older, lean is commonly recognized as a by-product of the Japanese automotive industry, notably Toyota in the later 1940s. It emerged as a continuous process for the improvement of the (continuous) production process.

Lean consists of five processes applied in a continuous loop. The first task is to identify value that the customer is looking for a process, e.g. a manufacturing or service management, to provide. Secondly, identify all the steps in the value stream, i.e. the process, and identify any unnecessary or inefficient aspects. Step 3 is to tighten up the process in all its aspects, for example, any pinch points. Step 4 is to identify the factors that establish what is called pull. Pull in operational process is something that will trigger the next step in the process. For example, you may manufacture various components, but you would not then move them to assembly until you have all the components required gathered and ready. Just in time came out of this.

By the end of Step 4, the latest efficiency level in the process has been gained so Step 5 then is starting the whole circle again. When going through the five steps of the lean process another lean technique is frequently brought to bear, which is Lean Six Sigma.

Example: Keep the coffee flowing
Some years ago, I had the huge pleasure of working with a wonderful company that imported both coffee machines and coffee. They supplied and maintained coffee machines to varied customers from independent coffee shops to chains to hotels and hospitality companies. As well as supplying coffee.

They had grown rapidly, which was causing some operational issues. I was asked to investigate and used the lean process flow.

Step 1: I interviewed both senior management in the company and some of their clients to determine what value and outcomes their customers wanted and, in some instances, were not receiving. I quantified this as far as possible such as through measured delay in supply and complaint frequency.

Step 2: Through interview, observation and documentation, I was able to produce a model of how the organization should be working and how it was actually working.

I combined Steps 3 and 4: My key conclusion was that each department was coherent within itself but the issues arose from the hand-offs between them. Such as machines brought in for maintenance when unable to be fixed on site.

1. An engineer brought a machine into the factory and logged its arrival on site.
2. The machine would routinely be placed in the warehouse as the workshop had no spare space.
3. The workshop received a notification from the engineer that a repair was required, but not where the machine was. This arose from when the company was smaller with lower work volumes and machines for repair went straight to the workshop.
4. The workshop knew to manage repairs within the timescale of a customer's Service Level Agreement.
5. But the workshop clock only started when they received the machine from the engineer or warehouse.
6. There was no rigid control of non-new machines into the warehouse. Sometimes it was difficult to discriminate between machines for repair vs. recycling/scrap.

The essential issue was a poor workflow for maintenance, plus an associated under-resourcing issue in the workshop. This had not been picked up due to the measured volume of work, which was 10–15% less than the true rate.

Step 5: Consisted of a monthly review of the workflow and resource usage in the workshop.

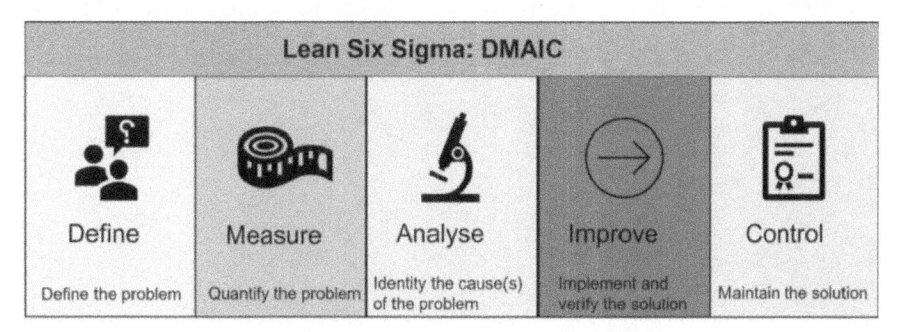

Figure A.2: Six Sigma model

Lean Six Sigma has five steps to it, as can be seen in Figure A.2, to *define* the problem. Then to *quantify* the problem, then *analyse* it for areas of inefficiency. Then to look for ways to *improve* against those inefficiencies and implement them. Finally, to *control* and maintain that new solution.

It is clear that lean has evolved, and is mostly used in relation to continuous processes in an organization, whereas agile has come out of finite period software development. It makes sense then to reserve lean for continuous process and agile for project-based activity, as a rule of thumb.

Example: Airport traffic analysis
I have seen this used at an airport to increase the number of take-offs and landings that could be achieved. Even a small percentage increase (this was well before the impact of Covid-19) would potentially increase annual revenue by many tens of millions of dollars.

Lean Six Sigma analysis identified and quantified in great detail the many factors that influenced take-off and landing timing. On the apron, e.g. controlling movement not just of aircraft but also vehicles (fuel lorries, baggage trains, buses etc.), plus regular runway inspections and so on. And in the terminals, such as passenger rates through security, passengers late to gates, loading times, periods of flight congestion. Plus air traffic control factors including competition for passage through airspace and holding pattern timings.

Both of these examples have been of business-as usual-operations – recurring operational business processes from which lean emerged and for which it is suited.

Acknowledgements

Firstly I want to thank a number of people, who through conversations with me have influenced this book and its contents. In surname order as they are all amazing practitioners: Professor Stephen Carver, Adrian Dooley, Sean Guinness, Dr David Hillson (the Risk Doctor), Stephen Jones, Steve Messenger and Steve Wake.

Adrian Dooley and Steve Messenger I also thank as my readers and Steve too for his Foreword.

To the many organizations and teams I have worked with, who have provided me with mostly great experiences, opportunities to learn and develop both my capability and ideas. Special thanks go to Lee Grant, CEO of Wrangu. Lee has been a client several times, a good influence, always a joy to work with and a friend throughout.

There are many people in my professional journey to whom I owe thanks, mostly many colleagues inside the Association for Project Management (APM), now and in the past nearly 30 years. Brian Wernham is thanked for his influence on my agile journey and for putting up with me during our agile roadshows.

My years working with ProgM SIG in APM were formative, at times combative but always creative. People from my era who greatly influenced me were John Chapman and the much-missed Paul Rayner. Both were also co-authors with me of the *Gower Handbook of Programme Management* (1st edition), along with Malcolm Anthony and Geof Leigh. Nor have I forgotten the man who led us and ProgM for so many years. This book is dedicated in part to the greatly missed father of programme management, Geoff Reiss.

The editor is the often-unsung hero for a book. In this case I certainly thank Jonathan Norman for his informed, direct and always constructively critical... critique.

Finally, this book is also dedicated to my partner of 30 years, Gordon, who has given me great support and at times just told me to get on and finish!

About the author

The project profession has been my home for more than 30 years. I describe myself as a project professional, a designation that did not exist in the 1980s. I have been fortunate to witness the fantastic evolution of the profession, and of playing my part.

My interest in methods, their evolution and adaptation commenced in telecoms with BT (British Telecom back then) as a trainer/internal consultant in business analysis, software design, development and project management. We even developed an integrated project management and software development method called Telstar. It grew out of PROMPT, a precursor to PRINCE2, and SSADM (Structured Systems Analysis and Design Method). Our ambition went as far as designing a toolset to automate much of Telstar. BT, probably sensibly, decided against the significant investment in development.

This stimulated me to become more interested in the profession and I joined the Association for Project Management in the early 1990s, becoming active in the emerging programme management special interest group, ProgM, led then by the incredible, creative and much-missed Geoff Reiss, for me *the* Guru of programme management. Programme management had evolved from the inability of project management methods to handle the increasing scale and complexity of change.

During my time with ProgM we carried the flame for other evolutions in the profession inside APM, notably portfolio management, project management offices, benefits management and increasingly the human aspects of the profession such as stakeholder management and communication.

I can proudly say that other SIGs emerged to greatly advance the early work of the ProgM team in the areas of PMOs, portfolio management and so on. ProgM continues to evolve and promote programme management actively and effectively.... without me to get in the way.

Six of us, again led by Geoff Reiss, published the first *Gower Handbook of Programme Management* in 2006. I slightly shudder to recall that Geoff Reiss, Malcolm Anthony, John Chapman, Geof Leigh, Paul

Rayner and I put more than 100 years' project experience into that book. I am sorry that there is only 30-odd years in this one.

From 1996 until about ten years ago I led or rescued transformation programmes well beyond telecoms in various industries and both commercial and public sectors, including: aviation, finance (retail, investment and lease), energy technologies, mining, video technologies, nano-technology, recruitment, software products, central and local government, the charity sector... and coffee!

I took on roles from project manager through to Head of Customer Projects, trouble-shooter, consultancy roles, e.g. the design/build/operation of P3 methods, and even wrote a report for the National Audit Office.

In parallel I have co-authored publications for APM and been a contributor and reviewer for government programme, portfolio management and PMO standards. I have lectured extensively in the UK, Europe and now online. This included the agile project management roadshow I did with Brian Wernham (Author: *Agile Project Management for Government*) for a couple of years. I remain a visiting lecturer at several business schools, notably for ten years at Nottingham University Business School.

And I am still learning.

Glossary

Given that the project management terms used in this book are consistent with the Association for Project Management's BoK 7, explanation of these terms will mostly not be included here but can be found in the Glossary of APM BoK 7.

Assumed (informal) authority: A person acts in a manner where a third party would assume that the person has the right to act.

Backlog: A list of everything to be done to build a complete product.

Business Operating Model: Describes how an organization creates, delivers and captures value and sustains itself in the process.

Emergent risk: An ontological uncertainty, risks that emerge from our blind-spots, the unknown unknowns.

Event risk: A possible future event which, if it occurs, will have an impact on the project's goals. Also called stochastic uncertainty.

Hands-off leadership: A form of control where the leader allows others to act on their own, but keeping sufficiently in touch to be able to intervene when they need to or are asked to.

Importance: The relative priority of a task.

Mindset: The established set of attitudes held by somebody that influences their thinking and behaviour.

Non-event risk: Where there is uncertainty in relation to some aspects of a task or outcome.

Non-supportive organizations: An organization whose policies, structure, processes or systems make it difficult for projects to operate.

Operating model: Describes how the business model will be delivered.

Organizational culture: Defined as the underlying beliefs, assumptions, values and ways of interacting that contribute to the unique social and psychological environment of an organization.

Organizational project management: A model that describes an integrated organizational culture in which both project-based and business-as-usual work can thrive.

P3: Acronym for portfolio, programme and project management.

Problem: A small issue that can normally be dealt with rapidly and informally.

Project economy: The movement towards the increasing use of projects to handle work and solve problems.

Project management framework: A documented architecture that defines how a project management method can be used in an organization.

Self model: A model which describes how individuals develop as a member of a team.

Sublimation: The degree to which an individual surrenders their self-interest to the interests of a team of which they are a member.

Supportive organization: An organization whose policies, structure, processes or systems enable projects to operate effectively.

Target operating model: A blueprint of how an organization's vision is supposed to align with its objectives and capacities.

Total quality management: An organization-wide philosophy with its core values centred on continually improving the quality of its product and services, and the quality of its processes, to meet and exceed customer expectation.

Uncertainty (in relation to risks): The degree to which one or more aspects of a risk are unknown or difficult to quantify.

Urgency: A measure of how soon a task must be done.

Notes

[1] Abrahamson, Eric (2004) *Change Without Pain*. Harvard Business School Press.

[2] PA Consulting (2021) *The Evolution of the Agile Organisation*.

[3] Project Management Institute (2020) Pulse of the Profession® report: *Ahead of the Curve: Forging a Future-Focused Culture*.

[4] Standish (2018) *CHAOS Report: Decision Latency Theory*.

[5] Association for Project Management (2015) *Conditions for Project Success*. Research report.

[6] Association for Project Management (2021) *Dynamic Conditions for Project Success*. Research report.

[7] Project Management Institute (2020) Pulse of the Profession® report: *Ahead of the Curve: Forging a Future-Focused Culture*.

[8] National Audit Office (2011) *The Failure of the FiReControl Project*. Report by the Comptroller and Auditor General, HC1272 Session 2010–12, 1 July 2011.

[9] Birkinshaw, Julian and Ridderstråle, Jonas (2015) 'Adhocracy for an agile age', *McKinsey Quarterly*, 1 December 2015.

[10] Regus (2017) *The Workplace Revolution: A Picture of Flexible Working*.

[11] Pullan, Penny (2016) *Virtual Leadership*, 1st edition. Kogan Page.

[12] Association for Project Management (2016) *Directing Agile Change*.

[13] Nason, Rick (2017) *It's Not Complicated: The Art and Science of Complexity in Business*. Rotman-UTP Publishing.

[14] Landry, Meredith (2013) 'Risk and reward', *PM Network*, 27(9), 44–49.

[15] O'Brochta, Michael and Robertson, Calum (2012) 'PMOs under pressure', *PM Network*, 26(4), 26–27.

[16] Nieto-Rodriguez, Antonio (2021) 'The project economy has arrived', *Harvard Business Review*, November–December.

[17] Abrahamson, Eric (2004) *Change Without Pain*. Harvard Business School Press.

Index

Note: Page numbers in *italic* refer to Figures; those in **bold** refer to Tables

7Ss organization design model 66

Abrahamson, Eric 6, 182, 183
adaptation 6, 84, 126, 160, 189
adhocracy 8, 68–69
agile 21, 31, 36–43, 193, 196
agile development 13, 39
agile development team 10, 39, 40
agile leadership 67–70, 80–82, 86, 181
    authority 74, 76–77
    hands-off leadership 70–77
Agile Manifesto, the 3–4, 5, 6, 9–13, 32, 68, 126, 127, 172
agile organizations 7
agile portfolio build 166–171
agile project management 2, 4, 14, 15–16, 17, 18, 31
agile project management maturity model 6, 183
agile projects 9, 14, 18–19, 31, 34–35, 36
agile project teams 82–85, 86
agile software development 4, 10–11, 14
agility 1–4, 5–6, 7–13, 17, 50, 55, 63, 191–192
airport operations 42, 76–77, 104, 110
airport project portfolio management 127–128, 168–169
airport traffic analysis 196
Apollo moon missions *146*, 147
approvals 12, 108–109
artificial intelligence (AI) 2, 3, 6, 26, 152

Association for Project Management (APM) 6, 25, 43, 47, 57–58, 89, 100, 179
assumed authority 76–77
assurance 13, 55, 56, 60, 162, 170–171
attention 42
audit trail 17
authority 18, 55, 76–77
    agile leadership 74, 76–77
    to spend 133–134

behavioural change 145, 189
behavioural manipulation 126
behavioural responsibilities 149
Birkinshaw, Julian 8, 69
British Telecom (BT) 46–47, 152, 160
BT PhONEday 96–97, 162
budget approval 133–134
business analysts 38–39
business-as-usual operations 27, 45, 53, 89, 102, 107, 165–166
business case 15, 17, 129–133, 134
business model 179
business planning 106–107, 108–109, 130
business transformation programme 106, 192

Cable & Wireless 155
Caesar, Julius 82
Capability Management Maturity Model (CMMM) 183, **184–188**, 189

capability management maturity
    models 191–192
Carver, Stephen 37
change 13, 14, 17, 63–64, 65, 182–183
change control 6, 14, 25, 61, 126–129, 172
change management 65, 171–174
coffee company 48, 194–195
collaboration 13, 14, 89, 116, 128
collaborative behaviours 18–19, 138, 149
communication 11, 98–99
communication planning 91–92, 95–98, 115
complex problems 123, 124, 126
complicated problems 123, 124, 126
contracts 13, 14, 142–143, 144–145
creative destruction 182
creative recombination 182–183
creativity 89–91
C-suite 31, 40–42, 52, 53, 68, 180, 181
culture 189
culture of agility 89–91, 103
customer satisfaction 16, 99

Daley, Tom 58
Department of Work and Pensions 116–117
digital businesses 8
disruptor companies 8
documentation 12, 13–14, 29, 38
Dooley, Adrian 29
Drucker Forum, Vienna 8, 48, 189

eight-stage change model 42, 43
emotional reactions 63–64
empowerment 18, 189–190
Energy Technologies Institute (ETI) 112–113, 116, 141
engagement 10–11, 17, 42, 70
    senior management 43
    stakeholders 100, 101

enterprise project management office (EPMO) 74, 153, 164, 165, 171, 174–175
escalation 123
executive level 31, 40–42, 52, 53, 68, 180, 181

fail fast 117–118
financial controls 129–130, 134–135
FIRe control programme 61–63, 97, 144
fit for purpose 146, 147
flexibilty 10, 17
frameworks 2, 5, 22, 24–25, 26, 29, 58–59, 61, 192
    Organizational Project Management Framework 54–55, 191, 192
    project management 59–61, 105

global mining company 111–112
governance 13, 55, 56, 60, 74, 105–106, 109, 112, 133

hands-off leadership 70–77, 105
    airport operations 76–77
    assumed authority 76–77
    supermarket change programme 72–76
high performance 191
high staff turnover 125
Hilson, David 118
homeworking 77–79
house builds 144

iceberg model, organizational culture 48, *49, 62*, 65, 68, 182, 190
Ikea 178–179
integrated model for project agility 3, *177*, 178, 191
investment finance programme 113
iron pyramid 24

iron triangle 23
issue management 118–119, 121–122, 123

just good enough 146, 147

Kanban (Lean manufacturing) 3
Kodak 63
Kotter 18, 42, 43, 63
    Kotter's eight-stage change model 42, 43

Landry, Meredith 129–130
leadership 70, 86, 149–150
    agile leadership 67–77, 80–82, 181
Lean 5, 21–22, 146, 193–196
learn and improve 146
lease finance delivery partner selection 140–141
London 2012 Olympics 126, 144–145

management by exception 74, 109, 115, 122
maturity models 52, 179, 183
Messenger, Steve 2, 63, 68
mindset 15, 41, 63, 68–69, 189
minimum viable product (MVP) 15–16
misinformation 191
mobile phone company 163–164
monitoring (tracking) 86, 109–110, 111
MoSCoW prioritization *169*
motivation 11
multi-year project/programme 108
MVP *see* minimum viable product (MVP)

nano-technology company 158–159
Nason, Rick 123–124
new operations 5, 101, 104, 107
NHS NPfIT email project 97–98

non-agile organizations 166
non-supportive organizations 52, 134–135, 157, 158

operating model 179
Opex vs. Capex 102
organizational agility 7–9, 191
organizational change 182, 188–189
organizational culture 6, 8–9, 47–52, 54–55, 61, 63, 64–66, 68–69
    iceberg model 48, *49, 62,* 65, 68, 182, 190
organizational landscape 5, 13, 18, 29, 45, 46, 53, 177, 191
organizational project management 3, 52, 53, 54–55, 163
Organizational Project Management Framework (OrgPM Framework™) 54–55, 191, 192
organizations 1, 2, 6, 191
    supportive 43, 52, 106, 134–135, 157–158
    unsupportive 52, 134–135, 157, 158
oversight (governance) *see* governance

PA Consulting 7
people 24, 189
People, Process and Tools model 22–25, *57,* 59–60
pitfalls 181, 191
planning 6, 24–25, 37, 53, 109–111, 113–114
PMI *see* Project Management Institute (PMI)
PMOs *see* enterprise project management office (EPMO)
portfolio management 6, 157, 163–171, 172–175
Powell, Colin 69
PRINCE (Projects in a Controlled Environment) 22, 23–24

PRINCE2 22, 24, 25, 28
problem solving 123–126
process adaptation 126, 189
procurement 139–145, 189
programmes 6, 157–162, 189
programme shaping 160–161
programme structure 160–161
project agility 1–6, 13–14, 21–29, 31, 110, 177–181, 188–190, 191–192
project-based activity 166
project delivery success 177
project economy 3, 46, 106, 163
project failure 1, 46, 191
projectization of work 2, 3, 6, 46–47
project landscape 26–28, 46, 47
project life-cycles 6, 10–11, 34–36, 148–149
project management 2–4, 5, 7, 13–14, 15–19, 28, 32, 34, 89, 191–192
project management agility 2, 3–4, 15–19, 22, 57
project management framework 59–61, 105
   People, Process and Tools model 22–25, 57, 59–60
Project Management Institute (PMI) 3, 7, 25, 43, 46, 47, 119, 163, 164
project management methods 24–25, 26, 105
project management tools 6, 154–156
project managers 39–40, 67
project organizations 6, 191
projects 1–2, 6, 19, 26–28, 45, 53, 86
project success 2, 26, 46, 177, 191
PROMPT (Project Resource Organization Management and Planning Technique) 22

quality management 147–149

Regus report 77–78
remote working 77–79

reporting 38, 109–110, 111, 112, 113–114, 115, 122, 123
resource management 101–103, 136–138
responsibilities 89, 149–150
retail transformation programme 128–129
Ridderstråle, Jonas 69
risk 117–122, 123, 132, 144–145, 189
roles 6, 16–17, 89, 149–150

Schein, Edgar 47–48, 65–66
Scrum 31, 32–34, 35, 39–40, 167
seat-back video aviation programme 122
security and data products company 107–108
self model 87–88
self-organizing teams 12, 86, 119, 123
senior management 19, 31, 42, 43, 106, 119, 123
shaping 160–161
Shell Project Academy 51–52
Six Sigma model 124, 194–196
software development 4, 7, 32
software tools 6, 151–156
spend, authority to 133–134
sponsors 53, 106, 134, 158, 159–160
stage gate process 148–149
stakeholder management 67, 91–95, 100–101, 189
stakeholders 172
   communications 189
   engagement 100, 101
Standish Group 9
strategic planning 106–109, 179
supermarket retail point-of-sale (PoS) programme 72–76, 148–149, 161
supportive organizations 43, 52, 106, 134–135, 157–158

talent management 103–104

team performance management 86
technology 151–156, 189
tenders 139–141, 142
third parties 138
   contracts 142–143, 144–145
   procurement 139–145
   risk 144–145
   tenders 139–141, 142
tools 25, 114, 151–156, 189
Total Quality Management (TQM) 146
traditional project management 28
transparency 115–117
trust 116–117

UK telco professional services 99, 145
unsupportive organizations 52, 134–135, 157, 158

urgency and importance 122

value 6, 7, 8, 9, 10, 12–14, 19, 179, 180–181
virtual working 77–82
vision 178–179
VMOST model (Vision, Mission, Objectives, Strategy, Tactics) 167–168, 179
von Moltke, Helmuth 171

waterfall life-cycle 9, 10, 35, 36
Wrangu GDPR app customer implementation 154–155

Y2K syndrome 164–165